THE
CUSTER WOLF

THE
CUSTER WOLF

Biography of an American Renegade

by ROGER A. CARAS

INTRODUCTION BY
GERALD DURRELL

ILLUSTRATED BY CHARLES FRACÉ

Holt, Rinehart and Winston · New York

Library of Congress Cataloging in Publication Data
Caras, Roger A
The Custer Wolf.
1. Wolves—Legends and stories.   I. Title.
QL795.W8C33   1979   599'.7444   78–14180
ISBN 0–03–016616–0

Original edition published by Little, Brown and Company
(Boston) and simultaneously in Canada by Little, Brown
and Company (Toronto) Ltd.

First Holt Edition: 1979
Printed in the United States of America
1 3 5 7 9 10 8 6 4 2

For Jill, who has wept for a wolf

INTRODUCTION

Together with many other forms of life the predators of the world—the leopards, tigers, bears, wolves, foxes, and so on—all face a fairly bleak future with their habitat being destroyed and every human being's hand against them. No predator has a good reputation and of all of them probably the wolf has the worst. Ever since Little Red Riding Hood the wolf has had a bad name, and this in spite of the fact that any little girl stupid enough to mistake a wolf for her grandmother deserves to be eaten.

Any animal that has the audacity to take what man considers to be his rightful prey—i.e. chickens or sheep or cows—immediately becomes classified as vermin, and as such must be extirpated wherever found. No thought is given to the biological necessity for predators. The harm of taking the odd chicken or sheep is never balanced against the good that the predator performs in rodent control or in keeping the numbers of a potentially numerous species, such as deer, in check. Time and again it has been proved that if you destroy all the predators in an area, be they mountain lion or wolf, the result will be a devastating population explosion among the rodents or deer. In Patagonia once the sheep farmers (who, all over the world appear to be men with intelligence as limited as the animals they farm) decided to have a massive death drive on the local foxes since they were occasionally guilty of stealing the odd lamb. So with the aid of poison, gun, and trap they exterminated the fox over a vast area. Immediately they found themselves faced with a much greater problem which they had created. The wild geese in the area had been the staple diet of the fox. Now, with no predator to keep them in check, there was a population explosion of some magnitude, so much so that the farmers found that the vast array of geese their interference had created were overgrazing the pastures, taking food away from the sheep. The farmers, in desperation, had to go through the ludicrous performance of replacing foxes on their pasture land as this was the only method of controlling the birds. All this because they did not realize how the fox fitted into the whole scheme of nature. The few lambs taken were, in fact, a very small "salary" when you considered the fox as a pest control officer.

In this brilliant and evocative book Roger Caras has not only shown us the wolf's role in nature, but he has also shown us how a wolf thinks and feels. It is very difficult to write a book like this without falling into the trap of anthropomorphizing the animals, making them think and feel like human beings instead of animals. But this is a trap that the author has triumphantly circumnavigated and has given us a deeply moving and beautifully written book. In a lifetime of reading books about animals I can count on the fingers of one hand the number that have been as well written and so delicately observed as this one. It is, in my opinion, a tour de force and should be on the bookshelves of anyone who is interested in animal life and fine writing.

GERALD DURRELL

THE
CUSTER WOLF

PROLOGUE

THE great tan wolf had not eaten for four days and nights. For that length of time he had crouched in the ravine with his head resting on the body of his mate. When her body had stiffened and grown cold, when it no longer rolled softly to his proddings, he had settled down to wait. He could not know what it was that held him there, but something within him forbade his abandoning the body with which he had only recently been joined—the body within which his cubs had died, one by one.

The tan wolf had been three years old when he had first encountered his mate below South Dakota's Rosebud Indian Reservation, across the line in Nebraska. At three, she was ready to mate, just entering the beautiful, rich prime of her life. Their meeting had been in the fall and they had approached each other slowly in an open field. He had picked up her scent two days before while stalking a stray prairie dog and had followed her cautiously, unsure of his own inner wonderings. When he finally swung in a wide arc across the open prairie so as to intersect her course she had slowed her pace not to overrun him. Ever since he had first come to know of her existence, ever since he plainted his first melancholy howl with muzzle to the sky, she had known. She had known and she had waited, patiently loping along with her tail held high in the easy flowing manner of the wolf.

There is a kind of wolf-etiquette that forbids the keeping of a stranger in doubt of his welcome. A wolf makes up his mind quickly and conveys his attitude to the approaching stranger. In this case, there was no doubt. The beautiful gray wolf had dropped down in her tracks, wagged her tail rapidly in the buffalo grass and rolled over from side to side. As befits the male wolf, the tan had crouched down a few paces off and watched her welcoming display. As she rolled over and back, again and again, he inched forward on his belly until her last roll brought her neck under his chin. He had rested his chin there for several minutes and then, with a quiet whining and humming, they had gotten up and trotted off together toward the north. After the manner of wolves, it was to be an arrangement for life.

In mid-February, after suffering the worst of the

thin winter together, the two became aware of a change in each other. The swellings and richenings within her own now-adult body were not understood by the she-wolf, but the stirrings they prompted were. She stayed closer than ever to her mate and engaged even more in the physical contact that had marked their meeting. They bathed each other endlessly, bit each other play-fully about the lips and muzzle. The tan wolf had done this from the very beginning, but now he held on longer, bit a little harder. Her response to the small pains of affection was no longer the slight warning growl. Now she whined, whined and moved closer, fre-quently throwing a foreleg over his neck until they rolled over and over each other. These gentle agonies summoned up the wolf within the wolf.

The male, too, felt the great difference. Unmated before, he was unsure of himself, but soon he came to associate her changing odor with his own longings. His feeling of fullness alternately irritated and lathered him into wild displays of puppy-like romping. It was the hoyden and the gamin.

One evening, just at sundown, the beautiful gray stopped in a frozen riverbed and refused to go on. She stood there waiting, knowing that which cannot be learned in a lifetime but only by the tutoring of eons. The male hurried up the embankment and gazed down at her, panting, his breath coming as miniature clouds of frost against the crisp winter dusk. He whined, he postured, he beseeched. Still she waited. Down on his haunches, the male put his chin to the sky and sent a long wailing aloft, sent it rolling across the sea of snow and wind-bared prairie. His ancient song tumbled across the frozen land, electrifying a hundred unseen ears. Two pronghorn moved swiftly over a ridge toward their distant herd, struggling in frozen drifts to keep their silhouettes away from the lowering sky. Again and again the tan wolf vented his call, the call of his ecstasy, while she waited patiently in the ravine. Satisfied with what his song had accomplished, his tribute paid to the night, the tan slipped down over the edge and moved slowly into the pool of shadows. His adolescence was now behind him and he could assume the role for which he was intended. Nearby a great owl thundered to earth and a trail of miniature tracks in the snow ended in a mass of wingbeats. A single drop of blood fell to the white crust, and a sacrifice was made to the night as the price of a new beginning.

Their joining unleashed new powers within the wolves. Instincts were freed from the prison of youth and the mated pair began to prepare for what was to follow. Less than twenty miles north of the ravine they found a site suitable to the needs of a home range. A natural cave was formed by an overhang that shadowed the bed of an ancient and forgotten river. The high ground above the ledge provided a sweeping view of miles of open prairie, while a clump of trees a quarter of a mile down the ravine from the cave provided emergency cover. A small pond at the foot of the rise, although now frozen, meant water on the days of the blistering prairie sun. The man-smell was not near, and so the wolves began to excavate their den.

Kills made near the ravine permitted the pair to continue their preparations. There were prairie dogs, rabbits, rarely a pronghorn, and once they happened upon a bull bison astray from his diminished herd. They were unable to wear the bull down and gave up after a determined charge by the horned one had nearly caused the death of the tan male.

Occasionally, sometimes for days on end, the wolves traveled far before they found food. At such times, little was accomplished at the den site; but by the time the gray wolf had completed forty days with the cubs inside her, the den was complete. The excavation ran sixteen feet into the embankment. The nesting chamber at the end of the tunnel was trampled hard and kept immaculately clean. The entrance was invisible unless one stood down on the floor of the ravine looking up.

Once the homesite was established, the male marked his boundaries. Circling the focus point at a distance of several miles, he watered small bushes and occasional rocks. Scraping small mounds of earth together, he wet on these, too, where the ground was flat. An unmistakable ring of scent now circled the cave and all animals would beware, for here lived the great tan wolf and his beautiful gray mate.

Less than two weeks short of the sixty-three days needed by the she-wolf to produce her cubs, the bad time started. The male was now going off to hunt alone. His mate was spending more and more time in the den fussing over the small details, smoothing the bed, or just sleeping. On one lone hunt the male found himself confronted with a new animal—one whose scent seemed strangely familar but did not trigger the recognition that would tell him how to hunt it. He could not know that this strange brown and white animal encountered at dawn was a milk cow that had wandered from a farm ten miles distant during a storm the preceding day.

The kill was quick and easy and the wolf gorged himself, keeping great hunks of meat free of digestion in the strange manner of these animals. When he reached the ravine and found his mate sitting by the entrance of the den, he easily retched up whole chunks of still fresh meat. The she-wolf ate hungrily while the male sat and watched her. The appreciative sounds she made in her throat as she feasted satisfied the male that he had done as he should.

After a day and half a night, the male prepared to return to the kill. There was a rubbing of noses and much tail-wagging and when the male set off his mate was with him. In the normal course of things it would have been the she-wolf's last hunt before retiring to await the coming of her cubs.

As they approached the kill the male slowed his pace. Over all there hung ominous warnings. Something was wrong. Nearby were two dead coyotes and there was the strange and distasteful man-smell and the smell of horses. Carefully, the male surveyed the prairie but could see nothing, hear nothing, that did not belong with the land. Growling softly, he smelled the now stiff bodies of the coyotes and turned to his less cautious mate as she fed on the baited carcass of the cow.

The male, unsure, stood off to the side trying to lure the she-wolf away from the kill. Suddenly the gray stopped feeding and leaped backward, bringing her forepaws to her muzzle. She shook her head and began to topple with a wild sound in her throat. Turning, she stumbled toward her mate, her jaw striking the ground as her front legs gave out. White saliva bubbled around her mouth and a strange look haunted her eyes. Her sides heaved as she fought to rid herself of the fatal meal, but the white powder that man calls *strychnine* had robbed her of this faculty. She seemed unable to walk and her mate, now excited beyond containment, tried to drag her toward a small ravine a few dozen yards off. Twice the she-wolf tried to get to her feet and twice she failed. Frantic to be gone from their exposed spot on the open prairie, the tan wolf tugged and pulled until he had his stricken mate out of sight in the ravine.

There he waited until she died. And there he waited for four more days and nights.

It was early in May when the tan wolf trotted out of the ravine and headed for the north. Twice he crossed boundaries he himself had marked and then he was gone from his private range. Once again he was a lone wolf searching for the companionship he must have to be complete. Stopping to hunt only for small animals— nestling birds, a dead badger, and once a rattlesnake—

he bypassed larger prey for the time it would have taken and pressed for the north. Three times he encountered the dread man-smell and quickened his pace until it was behind him.

Each night the wolf settled to his haunches and rolled his sadness across the land. It was no longer the call of an adolescent trying the strength of his throat, nor of a mated wolf triumphant in his completion. It was a questioning howl that started low and went very high. As the note dropped it was chewed until it came out almost as spoken words; it ended in his throat having accomplished nothing. Each night he waited and called again and again, but there was no reply. The yapping of a coyote and the yowling of a distant hound gave no answers. Such unwanted echoes did nothing to ease the loneliness.

One night in early June, across the line in South Dakota, the wolf's howl was answered from a ridge not far off. Again and again he made his call, sent his messages tumbling against the night, and again and again the answer came without hostility. The two wolves were joined by a third and for hours their song filled the spring night sky. Centuries rolled backward and a primeval time was re-formed out of the fogs and mists of the past. Toward dawn the tan settled down and waited. He had crossed the boundary marks of another male wolf and was within a private hunting range. The third wolf that had joined the chorus was a female and the tan waited for his welcome.

Shortly after the sun was free of the eastern rim of

the sky, two wolves trotted up the slight rise and sat down a few feet from where the tan lay watching with his yellow eyes. Alert to a possible challenge, he kept his chin on the ground and waited for the sign. The black male stood at last and wagged his tail. His silver mate followed suit, and soon the three animals were trotting back toward the den site of the mated pair.

As the trio approached the opening of the den, beside a tree stump in a small wood, the mouth of the tunnel exploded and five bundles of furious energy burst upon them. Unhesitantly the cubs jumped over and on them, nipping at their legs and foolishly trying to bring them forcibly to ground. Following the example of his hosts, the tan lay down and allowed the cubs to maul him. Their snarling and nipping was answered by affectionate licking, or by a warning paw that sent them squealing to the ground.

Thus, throughout the summer and autumn, the tan wolf hunted and lived with the mated pair and their cubs. He saw to their schooling and helped in the care of the rapidly growing young.

On their hunts through the extensive range established by the black male, the wolves frequently encountered the man-smell and once saw strange creatures moving swiftly along the skyline. On the day of the first snow, still several months before the black and silver wolves would mate again, the tan wolf joined the black male in a hunt. The female stayed behind with her cubs, assuming the role the tan had often filled as he watched the mated pair trot off together. Now it was the tan and the black who moved off, leaving first tracks in the young snow that barely covered the prairie.

Shortly after they were out of sight of the wood they encountered the man-smell. It was strong now, mixed with the smell of horses and dogs. The indiscriminate wettings of the hounds made no boundaries, told no story that could be understood. Such senseless waste, such careless use of a means of expression confused the wolves and they soon abandoned their efforts to decipher the signals.

Suddenly, as they passed by a hidden, eroded ridge, the air was split and the world exploded about their ears. The black wolf crumbled in his tracks and lay still. A raging, red pain tore along the tan wolf's left thigh and made his leg buckle momentarily. The cry of hounds filled the sky and explosion after explosion split the world apart until fear was all there was.

To his feet even before he had really fallen, the tan wolf stretched flat out in great leaps until his feet barely touched the ground. The pain of his wound rode him like a savage vise. He could hear the calling and the cursing of the men and he could hear the dogs coming closer as they were loosed from their leashes. Earth spurted in little puffs around him but fell behind as he gained distance. He ran in a great circle many miles wide, until finally the dogs fell off the trail one by one and returned whining to their masters.

It was still daylight, and so he hid in some brush waiting for the hours to pass. The blood flow had stopped but his leg was matted and stiff. After nightfall he moved painfully in the direction of the den, veering off several times to keep the line of his trail from being straight. After circling several times, he arrived at the wood when the moon was full in the sky. The silver wolf came out of the den questioningly, but the tan snarled a warning and she followed his limping form into the passage.

Deep in the den the pups were tumbled in the abandon of their sleep. The tan found a space and collapsed with his head between his paws. A softness came over him as the silver wolf began to lick his wound. As he slept he relived his day and his legs kicked convulsively and a rumble filled his throat.

Three months later the silver wolf accepted the great tan as her mate, and he lived with his adopted family throughout the winter, through the time of the healing, and into the spring. By the time the silver wolf was ready to bear the tan his young, the cubs were large enough to hunt on their own. Before the young were born, therefore, the silver wolf settled in her den and allowed her cubs and their adopted father to hunt for themselves and for her. One by one the five yearlings began to stay away for days and nights at a time. There was no sadness in this, for it was time to give birth again. By April, when the new cubs were born, only one yearling remained at home—and the day after the birth, this yellow she-wolf also moved off, never again to return.

Five cubs were born in that cave beneath the stump

of the tree. One died and was carried off by the tan wolf. Of the four that remained, one appeared somehow different from the rest. He was white, and men would come to know him well and call him by a name that would live in history. For this was the beginning of the Custer Wolf.

ONE

As from a long sleep, the little wolf—the white one, last of five to be born in the cave beneath the great tree stump—struggled into consciousness. Exhausted from the pulling and crushing, worn out from the first great battle for survival, the little blind animal felt the air rush into his lungs, felt the strangeness of dry air against his nose and throat. Then he slept.

Not much more than a handful of fur, still soaked with the fluids of birth, the small creature felt the joy of movement, experienced the first ecstasy of freedom. Even as he slept his legs twitched and his head turned from side to side. After a few minutes the cub awakened, his whole being possessed with a desire he had not experienced before. There was a gnawing, a need to be filled, a need to press his muzzle and gums against something. He had to suck.

Instinctively he twisted and turned, trying to use his legs that were now free. Finally, driven by the strange mounting need, he crawled on his flat belly toward the source of heat, felt the fur, nuzzled it, searched through it. Something pressed against him, trying to push him back from the fur and warmth, but he struggled mightily against his littermates until he reached his mother's body. His nose found a hard little nipple and greedily he pressed himself to it, took it into his mouth and began working his gums. The rich, warm fluid poured into his mouth and he choked. Fighting back against his brothers and sisters, and fighting the great choking at the same time, he finally cleared his throat and mouth and sucked again. This time the fluid flowed properly, and for the first time in his life he swallowed. The aching in his guts stopped. The little white cub had won the second battle of his life. Here, in the hole beneath the ground, he would survive.

Sometime during that first day the wolf cub had a second great awakening. Strange sensations registered on his growing consciousness. With his nose pressed against the fur on his mother's belly, he received an impression that quickly shaped itself into his first memory. The next time he sought the source of warmth and food, there was no need to press into the fur to know that he was close. For now his nose directed his movements. He had the power of scent.

There were other things in the cave besides the fountain of warmth and milk. Something caressed him, cleaned his fur and made it smooth. This was the good feeling, the feeling that went along with the one that stopped the hurting in his belly. Each time he ate, he slept, and when he awakened he felt new strength in his legs. His muscles were filling out and he began to show a measure of coordination. Each time he tried a movement now it came easier. Soon he could crawl to his mother, over and across his struggling littermates, without difficulty. Hour by hour the strength came, and hour by hour the world formed into a reality.

For twelve days, the wolf cubs lived in a world of total darkness. There was no day, no night, only the need to fill their stomachs and the need to sleep. There was the warmth when they were near their mother, and the cold when they weren't. There was that which felt good, and that which felt bad. The great struggle was to achieve the one and fight off the other; as the hours and days progressed, the fight developed from an unconscious one to a conscious experience. Theirs was a completely elemental world composed of life-essentials.

On the thirteenth day a strange thing happened to the cubs. They kept turning their heads involuntarily toward that part of the cave from whence the cold air came. A strange magnet seemed to draw their attention toward the opening. Then, as their sealed eyes slowly began to open, a new sensation was given to them. Suddenly, quite suddenly, there was a light time and a dark time. At first, there was little to be seen, little that could not be recognized better by sound, touch, taste, and odor. Soon, though, there were things that could be separated from others by sight. When the large wolf— the one that did not offer the milk—returned to the cave, when his great form filled the mouth of the tunnel, it could be known because the light was cut off. Indeed, the first visual knowledge the cubs had was of the coming and going of their parents.

Now the world was very real. It could be tasted (by the end of the first week any foot or tail that came close was gummed and mouthed endlessly); it could be smelled; it could be heard. And now, it could be seen.

For four long weeks the cubs were restricted to their tight little world beneath the tree stump. Smells and even some muted sounds drifted toward them from the mouth of the tunnel as their parents moved in and out of the blinding light, but any move in that direction by a cub brought a warning growl from one or both parents. Those cubs that ignored the growl the first few times quickly learned that a law existed that governed their lives.

One morning both parents left the cave together. The cubs could hear them outside whining, making little calling sounds. Hesitantly they stumbled and rolled over each other toward the sound. Suddenly the father loomed in the light, walked over them, bowling their round bodies against the sides of the tunnel. He turned in the end chamber and began pushing from behind. One against the other, the cubs were tumbled and pushed until they were at the mouth of the tunnel. One by one they felt the searing pain as the hot light crashed against their eyes and blinded them.

Strange odors, strange sounds unheard before, and hot light bombarded them. They whined and turned to re-enter the safety of the tunnel—all but one. The white cub stood alone at the entrance, his forelegs stiff, braced against the world. A baby cry, an approximation of a growl, filled his throat.

Meanwhile, the parents picked up the other cubs in their jaws and gently carried them to the flat place in front of the tunnel mouth. Individually they were retrieved from the tunnel to which they tried desperately to return and were carried again to the world outside. The white cub stood braced until he too was scooped up and carried to the flat place. Tumbled together, cowering as the world exploded its new sensations against them, the cubs huddled and whimpered, each trying to hide under the others. The suspicion and fear with which they reacted to the new world was infectious and the small, round bundle of white fur that was Lobo whimpered with the rest.

After the first fearful minutes, a new sensation, a new need filled the cubs. They were curious. Despite their fears, despite the threat of the bird sounds in the trees and the wind sounds, they began to investigate. Hesitantly, each turned from the group and began to seek the secrets of this strange new world. Each new sound electrified them and sent them tumbling toward each other. Slowly they became oriented and their curiosity, a passion that would be with them for as long as each lived, took over. Proudly, the parents stood off to the side and watched the awakening.

Within a matter of hours the cubs were rolling in

their tumbling games on the flat place. New sounds continued to distract them, but the terror was gone. This was the world to which they belonged. Once the white cub—Lobo—wandered off from the rest and heard the warning growl. Ignoring it, he continued toward the new smell that lured him. Suddenly his father loomed over him and the great mouth closed on his neck. He was jerked off the ground and roughly dropped back among his littermates. This was not the gentle carrying, but a stern punishment for not heeding the warning growl. In the few days that followed, the punishment became more severe, the teeth bit harder into the scruff, and the cubs learned that the warning growl was absolute.

Each day a signal—half whimper, half soft, rumbling growl—told the cubs that they might go to the flat place. And each day a quick growl told them to return to the tunnel. Outside they were allowed to investigate, to move off in new directions for a brief time; the warning growl told them when to stop and turn back, when to lie down, when to follow. Day after day the cubs learned to respond more quickly, came to know more signals, more directing sounds.

There were good times with the grown wolves as well. The tan male would lie down among them in the warm sun and invite them to torment him. They chewed and they snarled, they crawled on him and bit his ears. Patiently the male wolf tolerated their antics; but when he gave his warning signals, compliance must be immediate.

The mother, too, demanded total obedience. Her teeth were sharp, and the press of her great paw was painful on the neck. Together, the parents completed lesson number one in the education of the cubs.

Often the father moved off and was gone for hours at a time. When he returned he would deposit great smelly chunks of meat at his mate's feet. With a satisfied sound in her throat, the female would lie down and gnaw at her food while the male went off with the cubs for the tumbling and fighting games. One day (the cubs' thirty-fourth day) the father brought a small strip of meat to where the cubs were playing and dragged it before their noses. The white cub grabbed at it and began to shake his head, flopping the piece of meat back and forth. The little black female grabbed the other end and began to pull. A mighty tug-of-war was mounted and there was much baby snarling. The harder the white cub pulled, the deeper he sank his needle-sharp baby teeth into the meat.

Suddenly a juice flowed into his mouth and he let go of the prize, sending his sister tumbling end over end. He walked over to where she had dropped the meat and pawed it. He whined and cocked his head from side to side, sniffed it, and ran over toward his father, who was basking in the sun watching the antics. Arching his back, the white cub again stalked the prize; stiff-legged he jumped and rolled over it. Again he bit at the meat. The juice was strange and he ran to his mother and began to suck until the milk had washed the strange taste from his mouth.

Each day their father brought the cubs strips of meat to play with, and each day the games with them grew fiercer. There was the tugging, the pulling and the snarling. The meat could be charged, it could be run with, it could be torn from the grasp of another. But always there was the juice, the taste that came full and rich to the tongue. After a few days the taste was no longer strange. One by one, the cubs learned to gnaw on the prize once it was won from the others. Each time the supply of meat was bigger until there was enough for all.

After a few more weeks—about ten from the time of the birth—the cubs were eating a little meat each day. They still relied to a large measure on their mother's milk, but it was no longer enough. On some days great chunks of raw meat were carried to them by their father within his stomach; arching before them, he would retch the meat up, still fresh, still rich with the juice. On other days there would be a whole animal—a prairie dog or a squirrel—still in its fur. But before such prizes could be ripped apart and eaten, there must be the games; for the meat with the fur still on offered the greatest opportunity for the fighting play.

Always the eyes, the great yellow eyes of the parents, were on them. Always they were watched and often they heard the sound signals, the growls and low throat rumbles, to which they responded. Everything they did had a lesson behind it. In their eating, in their playing, in their very existence, the lesson was always there. One day, while they all lay about the flat place sleeping in the sun, the father leaped abruptly to his feet. The hairs along his back and neck stiffened and his back arched. Motionless he stood with his ears erect and his front legs braced. Suddenly he whirled and growled deeply—the warning sound. There was no allowance in the sound this time, no permissiveness. The female shot toward the mouth of the tunnel and echoed the warning. The cubs stumbled toward her, frolicking over and under each other in mock play. A second time the growl came and the father bit hard on the flank of the small tan male who was slower than the rest. The parent wolves rushed the cubs down the tunnel, herding them into the far chamber. The bodies of the adults blocked the passage, the female on the inside, the male pressed flat near the tunnel entrance, motionless, waiting.

A strange sound began to fill the world. A great thumping resounded through the tunnel and small bits of earth, the dust of the dried walls, filtered down. One of the cubs began to whine and a harsh grunt from the mother cut him short. Terrified, the cubs huddled in the chamber until the great rhythmic pounding faded off. The white cub felt the strange excitement of danger, felt the electricity that ran through his parents; he tried to crawl forward to where his father lay frozen, but a snarl from his mother sent him back to the others.

For the rest of the day the cubs were kept in the tunnel. Their movement was severely restricted and any effort to begin playing was cut off with a growl. For hours they lay in the chamber, until their mother finally came back and stretched out, allowing them to feed. They dropped off to sleep after filling themselves, the great adventure of the day soon forgotten.

The white wolf, the one we call Lobo, did not know that he had had his first encounter with his one and eternal enemy: man.

T W O

ALTHOUGH the wolf family reigned where they lived—as lords immune from intrusion or insult by other animals—their story was part of a greater one. Their lives revolved within a natural world that had many parts, all interconnected, many tied directly to the daily routine of the tan wolf, his she-wolf, and their four remaining cubs. They were part of a plan too vast for them ever to comprehend. Indeed, it is difficult enough for the mind of man.

The same spring that saw the birth of Lobo and his littermates saw many other new lives emerge as well. From the small shrews and moles and their very secret ways to the mysterious bats—the long-eared and the

hoary, the fringed and the red—from these small animals that flew first in the dying hours of the sun, from
all of them to the meddlesome raccoons, the fierce little
weasels and mink, the skunks, the feisty badger, the
foxes, and the clever little brush wolf that people call
coyote, all belonged to and were as much a part of the
world as Lobo and any of his kind. In his days, as they
stretched out before him, Lobo would have to learn the
elusive ways of each of these other creatures; he must
learn which to hunt and which to avoid. He would come
to know well the snarling bobcat, their deadly foe for all
time, whose lair was in a cave on higher ground and who
was as attentive to her cubs as the she-wolf was to hers.
Each hunted the same game and each would destroy the
other's cubs given the chance, so each was on guard
against the other. Their hatred better suited the cat,
but was blind and overburdening in both.

There were many animals in the world of the wolf
that served as prey—his for the asking, easily killed
and good to the taste. The ground squirrels, both the
spotted and the thirteen-lined, could be had by the
skilled wolf and would sustain life. The least chipmunk
served not as well because of his extremely small size,
while the black-tailed prairie dog was better with his
sassy, fat haunches. The plains pocket gopher, the
northern, the silky pocket mouse, the hispid, the kanga-
roo rat and the grasshopper mouse, these too could be
taken by the swift and the determined and could feed
the fires of the wolf's life force. There were still other
animals. Mice, like the white-footed and the deer;

beavers and bushy-tailed wood rats; voles of many
kinds, muskrats and jumping mice; the dangerous porcupine, tempting, but to be avoided; hares and rabbits—all these small creatures had their places. Larger
animals, too, filled gaps in the natural balance of the
world: mighty elk, more properly known as wapiti, appeared on rare occasions; swift mule deer and shy white-
tailed deer that became aggressive from late September
on when brown fluids oozed from the eye corners of the
antlered bucks; a few scattered bison; the incredibly
alert pronghorn (called antelope by the unknowing);
and, in the very high places, the tough and unforgiving
bighorn sheep. These furred animals, all kin to the wolf,
and the birds (those that nested high and those that
nested low and could be taken) and the reptiles, turtles,
lizards and snakes—some harmless, some deadly—these
too had their places in the world whose center was the
wolf. Each creature was in fact the self-appointed center of a private universe so that each revolved around
the other. The sum total of this apparent confusion, of
this giant kaleidoscope with uncounted dimensions, was
and is an order grander than all others: life itself.

Incredibly, before the tan wolf and his silver mate
could rest content in the knowledge that another generation had joined endless history, the cubs had to be
taught the ways of each animal. To survive, the young
wolf must know all basic facts, must have on file ready
for immediate recall the scents of each creature that he
might encounter. He must know that while his brain is
faster than that of a prairie rattlesnake his body is

slower, and he must learn to balance these facts in each encounter he might have with the legless ones—and there are many in the life of a wolf. The spray of the skunk can make him miserable and ill and can mark him with a smell that will last for months and make hunting extremely difficult; this too the cubs had to be taught. The tender pork flavor of the porcupine is dangerous to seek, and the cubs were taken near one and warned with urgent throat sounds that this must be forbidden them. Although the actual account could not be conveyed, the tribal memory of wolves curled up in their dens, dying in agony with their muzzles and paws festering in great open sores bristling with porcupine quills, was important for their well-being. Each lesson carried with it the urgency of survival. There was no waste. Each moment was profound.

And so, as the bosom of the earth warmed to the sun and began to give off its odors and its strength, a new year and new tasks opened before the wolf family. Spring, the sensuous season, the hedonistic one, had arrived and the earth had renewed its annual orgy. In the high places, the ponderosa pines began to grow again, giving off a turpentine odor as their orange twigs reached outward. The migrating Rocky Mountain juniper smelled tangy and offered hiding places to ground squirrels that strayed from their dens. The triple-leafed maple (called box elder), the swamp ash and water birch, the bur oak and maternal elms, the balsam poplar, eastern hornbeam and the cottonwoods, the hackberries, aspens and birches, each in its chosen place, each in places best for this very special reason or that, sucked at the soil, drank of the firm, warm breast of the earth and reached toward the sky with renewed strength. Their zest, their tangy fullness and richness added to the lives of all the creatures around.

The feathered ones were there, too. There were those who had wintered in the sheltered places nearby, who flew with renewed vigor, their stomachs newly full. There were those who had wintered far, far away, and who returned with whispered secrets to share among themselves on branch limb and other high and taunting places. The grebes—the eared, the western and the pied-billed—were on the lake. The herons were back, the great blue, the green, and the black-crowned night, adding to the stature and dignity of the scene. Bitterns, geese, and the ducks had also returned, along with the hawks—sharp-shinned and red-tailed, broad-winged and rough-legged, and goshawks. The marsh hawk, the osprey, and the prairie falcon had rejoined the raiders of the sky in partnership with the ubiquitous sparrow hawk. Pheasant, partridge, quail and crane added to the richness of the time and the place. Dozens of lesser songbirds, each as much a parcel of life as the wolf himself, flittered and enriched the scene, sang and gave testimony to life and eternity. In their challenges and gossip, in their unending elocution lurked many a symphony, many a poem. Thus each animal set about its task—life—for perpetual life is the responsibility of each creature. It is given in trust and must be passed on, a ringing truth that throbs in all living flesh.

The wolf is part of this total, of course, but a special

part: he is a predator. He cannot eat the leaves, herbs, and blossoms; he cannot suck nectar and create honey like the bee. The insect will not satisfy him as it will the bat; nor will bark do him any good, for he is unlike the porcupine. Grubs may save the shrew from certain starvation within hours, but the wolf could not survive on such fare. Like the cats, the weasels, and certain of the greater birds, the wolf requires more substantial fare.

Because the coming of the Custer Wolf was foretold by the genius of nature's secret knowledge, the world was ready, things were in balance, matters were in hand. Lesser creatures would bear more young than was needed by their kind, fecund mothers would bring forth an excess designed by millions of years of experience to feed this cub, even as it grew to adulthood. There would be more whitetail fawns, more rabbits and hares, even more birds than needed. There would be an excess of hundreds of thousands of mice in each square mile and these would sustain snake, owl, hawk, and wolf alike when need be. Their weeding out would be the predators' gift to the land. Nature was in harmony, even with its thousand thousand deaths, and there was nothing cruel, nothing savage, harmful or tragic in all this. No rabbit ever dies of old age, and none expects to.

The animals that eat the flesh of plant life have relatively little to learn. They quickly come to know the edible from the impossible and from that moment on their food problem is solved for life. Their only real worry is the predator—the snake for some, the great birds for others, the wolf for most. But even here, the tricks are few and repetitious and the lesson broad-based. These lesser animals learn to dread all movement, all shadows, all strange sounds and smells. Their small brains cannot separate foxes from wolves, hawks from eagles, so all are feared and avoided. That learned, the rodent, even the hoofed animal, can go about its way bolstered by instincts in quarters where education would have failed.

The problem for the predator is a different one. His education is elaborate, his preparation extensive. Left to his instincts he would die. He must know his fellow creatures much more thoroughly than they know him. He must know which challenges to accept and which to avoid. He must know how to feint with a large and potentially dangerous adversary and see how he hooks his horns. Like the matador, the wolf must study his potential prey and know where to put his body in those critical last seconds before his jaws close on the elk's throat. More than one poor student from a wolf litter has ended up feeding the ravens and other carrion seekers, his sides slit open, his body mangled by his intended prey.

Although the greatest danger facing an inexperienced or careless wolf is starvation, there are specific dangers in the taking of certain prey. Instinctively, the silver and the tan wolf both knew that they had this one year to teach the four cubs most of what they must know. When winter came, the cubs would be approaching proficiency, but they would stay close to their parents for months beyond the initial training period. The adults, however, could not continue to feed a family of four growing youngsters once the hunting went bad, when the snow came and many creatures went underground or left entirely. By the time winter came, the cubs would have to be contributing members of the polite and efficient wolf society.

Now that the cubs were in part dependent on meat and their education had begun in earnest, the silver wolf and her tan mate were bringing them out of the den each morning and allowing them to return only at night, when the weather turned bad, or when danger threatened.

Each day the excursions became longer, the exploration of the surrounding world more intense. Into fields where flowers grew in wild profusion the cubs were led and allowed to gambol like the fawns they would soon hunt. Into wooded patches near river banks they were led and shown how to find the path other animals used to and from the water. Through swamps and marshes their basic education took them, where musty plants and skunk cabbage grew. On highlands where the view encompassed all, on slopes where their silhouettes were held below the critical level of skyline, through every type of landscape, and therefore through every type of prey animal habitat, they were led. Sometimes they were permitted freedom to run and play; at other times, sharp calls or low rumbles herded them into line and cut short their frolicsome moods. Obedience had been learned, now all else would follow.

Once, as the wolf family emerged from a slashed and eroded ridge and stood on high ground overlooking a swampy lowland, the tan male gave a warning sound that brought the four cubs sharply to their senses and quickly to his side. He gave the unmistakable quieting sound and the cubs settled down until further instructions would tell them what to do. As the male settled the cubs down, the female began moving off slowly into the lowland brush and soon disappeared.

The male wolf went to each of his cubs in turn. Loving with his mouth, after his kind, he ran his tongue between their lips, tasted the roof of their mouths, and allowed them to return the favor. Quietly, methodically, he mauled each one briefly, licking, biting, pinning with paw, and then tasting the mouth. Each cub in turn squealed quietly, held his place, and was thus reassured by his parent.

When the male went down into the swampy place to join his mate in a hunt that would at once supply needed food to the family and serve as a demonstration of technique, he left behind four cubs content in their place in the world, sure of their parents, secure in the feeling if not the knowledge of being wolves. Here, again, was complex language. It was the vocabulary of the ear position and mane, the syntax of the tail.

From their vantage point the cubs could follow most of what happened, and all that was important. Some hundred yards ahead of where their mother had gone into the brush there suddenly exploded a whitetail doe. Swift and nimble she cleared a patch of brush and reached a brief stretch of open ground. Bounding to the

next patch she arched again, then again and then
again. Like music, like poetry, the graceful doe flowed
over each obstacle with a rhythm and an ease known
only to her. Meanwhile, streaking close behind, the she-
wolf kept the doe on the run. Nowhere near as nimble as
the deer, yet beautifully smooth and sure, she kept up
the pressure.

At the point where the doe could lose the silver wolf,
where her pursuer's stamina would give out, the tan
male suddenly bounded into view and took up the chase,
slowly working the doe around in a circle. In the mean-
time, the female cut across the arc and intersected the
doe's path at the point where the male was about to give
out.

The doe, her stamina now sorely tried, kept up her
gallant flight. Her leaps were less well-timed now, her
landings rougher. Several times her front legs came
close to giving out on impact and she nearly fell. Switch
after switch was made, the male wolf relieving his
mate, and then the female again taking her turn. What
they lacked in stamina and speed the wolves made up in
brains. Neither wolf, alone, would have been able to
take this deer. She was a prime animal and very fast.
Only her own blundering, her own inability to interpret
what the wolves were doing to her, would cause her to
fall prey.

All this the cubs could see, and from it they learned.
Moving back and forth with excitement, but always
within a few feet of where their father had left them,
they whined with frustration at being denied access to
the game. But they did not disobey.

Finally the whitetail took her last bound. Clearing some immature trees she came to earth, crumpled, and rolled over several times. The she-wolf was at her throat before she could right herself, and before she could give that first convulsive kick the male had hamstrung her —cut the tendons in her hind leg—making it impossible for her to regain her feet should the female lose her grip. The struggle soon ceased and the two wolves lay panting across the body of their prey.

There was no hate in the wolves' deed that day, and no cruelty. They did not enjoy a bloodbath in the way a human hunter who might have killed the same deer would have. There was no viciousness, no lust, no release of blind, frustrated fury, no such human emotions. There was hardly much choice. The wolves did just what they had to do. There were young to feed, as well as their own complaining stomachs, and a lesson to be taught.

The silver female left her mate with the kill and went for the cubs. As she came among them they ran about her, jumping up to tug at an ear and bite at her lips. She turned back and started toward the kill with two cubs gamboling on ahead, turning every few feet for approbation, and with two others hanging onto her perpetually tattered tail with their sharp and efficient little teeth. When she had had enough, she growled once and sent them all streaking on ahead toward their father, still resting on the kill.

When the family had assembled around the carcass of the doe the feeding began. The adults chose an area—the father at the belly, the mother at the throat

—and began to work at the hide. Mouthfuls of hair were pulled free and soon raw flesh was exposed for the feeding. The cubs, inexperienced with a whole carcass, worked first here and then there, getting little for their trouble except hair. The parents finally made room for them at the great holes they had opened up and the cubs were allowed to fill from the first great kill they had witnessed. That night they would remain away from their den for the first time.

Glutted, covered with gore and blood, they were subjected to an endless cleaning by the mother under some brush where the tan male had decided to hole up with his family for the night. They were no more than ten yards from the kill and the father lay watching it with his great yellow eyes barely blinking. The young were too full even to chase the raven that came to sit on the carcass and peck out bits for itself. A yapping coyote on a distant hill announced the coming of the night, and for the first time in their young lives the wolf cubs would go a twenty-four-hour period without suckling. Once or twice in their dreams their lips and mouths would make the motions, but they would be well supported through the night by the great piles of meat slowly dissolving in their bloated bellies.

Far away, under a bush, frozen into immobility by the earlier command of its mother, a fawn awaited her return. Without scent, blended into its hiding place by its spotted coat, the fawn would wait throughout the night, not making a sound. By morning its hunger would get the better of it and it would stand shakily and look about with fear in its eyes. At that moment a bobcat would be passing en route home to her cubs after an unsuccessful night's hunting. Intent on finding a vole or two to carry home, the she-cat would happen upon the fawn and the bobcat cubs safe in their lair would be fed. This is a drama older than the conscience of man by millions of generations and no one can profitably question it.

THREE

EVEN after witnessing their first major kill, even
after several subsequent adventures that opened
their lives to new dimensions, the cubs were a long way
from achieving any kind of independence. Puppy sub-
missiveness still marked their every move and controlled
the nature of every relationship into which they could
enter. Not until he is close to a year old does a wolf
begin to assume the air of authority. Until that authority blossoms, however, he is but partially a wolf.
Although it is born inside him as surely as his bones and
blood are, he must achieve it, earn it with his years.
Strangely, this authority, this fullness of being in a
wolf, is instinctive. Whereas he must learn so many of

the essentials of life, he has his "wolfness" within him by nature. This nothing can deny him—not captivity, not death. In the center of his yellow eye, in the core of his complicated brain and the fiber of his heart, a wolf is a wolf and can be naught else.

The cubs were not as concerned with their wolfness as they were with each succeeding instant of their life. Like children everywhere they were full with the adventure of living, fairly bursting with the need for expression. Each item on the agenda, parent-planned or cub-discovered, was a miracle, a source of boundless joy, for as long as it lasted. It was as much this shortness of attention span as anything else that marked the cubs' immaturity. A mature wolf can watch and wait for hours, a cub not yet fully a wolf cannot. To him, a pebble is a diamond for a few moments; or a newly found feather becomes the sole thread on which the entire universe is suspended. Once the feather is destroyed and the world fails to crumble, new avenues must be found—a butterfly perhaps. Many of the smallest creatures—the grasshoppers and moths, the nestling birds and the mice—must die before a predator is full born into the ways of his kind. A predator's emergence from infancy is a road paved with the carcasses of living sacrifices required in his education. To the cub of the wolf every living creature capable of being killed is an educational toy.

One day, in the course of an excursion, Lobo was basking in the sun, enjoying the grooming nibbles of the still attentive silver she-wolf. As he had grown he

had become less tolerant of her sometimes rough jaw-
ing, but he was still obedient and sat for the full course
of treatment. As his mother wandered away to groom
another cub, Lobo saw something move not far off.
Movement in the natural world is constant, but his
rapidly developing senses told him that the source in
this instance was an animal larger than any he had
handled alone before. Not without mixed feelings (one
of them fear), he began his stalk in the direction of the
disturbance. His muscles tightened under his skin and
the heavy fur along his back and over his shoulders
began to bristle. He wanted to whine, to yap his puppy
sounds, but his training held true and he remained
silent as he slipped forward, his belly barely off the
ground. His father sat on slightly higher ground and
watched his every movement, studying his technique.

Near where the wolves lay there was a heap of
rotting wood. Melting snow had left little pools in
cracks and dents that helped the process of decay. On
this rich garden there grew spicy tufts of the velvet-
stemmed collybia, the tangy early mushroom of spring-
time and dead wood. The sticky, reddish-yellow caps
with their tawny margins and the firm, velvety stems
arose from death but heralded new life and beauty. Attracted by the aroma of the collybia but surely immune
to its true beauty were two spicebush swallowtails. Relatively rare so far west, these four-inch butterflies
skidded low to the ground, changing from blue to green
in iridescent waves of living light as the sun's intensity
was filtered and changed by the foliage overhead.

Softly coming to rest near the mushrooms, they had become the focal point of another's attention.

The thirteen-lined ground squirrel was nearly a foot long, although four to five inches of that length consisted of unimpressive tail. As the name implies, his body was marked with thirteen lines, yellowish-white alternating with tones of chestnut, the darker punctuated with white spots. His face and underparts were a tinted buff that appeared first one tone and then another as his nervous movements constantly altered his relationship to light and shadow on the floor of the glade. His tail was yellowish-brown, fringed with coarse black hairs, each endowed with a yellow tip. He was as beautiful as he was nervous: a shadow, a dart, a flicker, a spot of life as he stalked the swallowtails. His great oval eyes saw all within immediate range—but they had missed the larger scale.

And so here was a moment in time, an infinitesimal microcosm in a world suspended somewhere between dinosaurs and space travel, a drama not only as old as time but reflecting the very essence of time itself. Here had germinated a seed and grown a tree tall and proud and here it had died after the nature of things. The elements had construed to pulp the wood, flake the bark, dissolve the chemicals and the stuff of its once impressive height and girth. On this decay a fungus grew, the spicy, scented collybia. The collybia, in turn, had drawn to it two mites of life, two wood nymphs in the persons of the swallowtails. In turn, stalking them, came the ground squirrel. His diet, half animal, half plant, had room in its range for these wisps of life, and he, this gentle creature of the daylight hours, became the hunter. Perhaps in justice, the turncoat squirrel was in turn hunted by the wolf cub—not so much in need of food as of experience.

Although he was in his spring weight—no more than four or five ounces—the squirrel had one very important element in his favor: a collection of twenty-two teeth, the front ones honed fine and sharp, ready for cutting. He also had a tenacity as rich and wonderful as that of the wolf cub—he wanted to live. He could not comprehend life, not even self; but in a finer, more precise wisdom, he wanted to maintain it. Here, surely, is another miracle we must acknowledge. Witless ones, unable to so much as begin to comprehend the existence of life, will nonetheless perform stupendous feats of bravery and heroism to defend it.

And thus the wolf cub came closer, not only to the squirrel but to the knowledge that life was not to be easy. Here was food—prey—that had to be taken; and although being a wolf might be the grandest miracle of all, it was not necessarily enough. You had to be a skilled wolf to survive, not just a wolf.

The consciousness of a ground squirrel, in matters of survival, does not deal in subtleties. He is either apprehensive or terrified, there is no other course. As the little animal moved in on the swallowtails, as intent as he was on his game, he was also alert to danger to himself. A sudden shadow could mean a hawk overhead, a rattlesnake striking from a tuft of grass, a fox or weasel, a coyote—even a wolf. For the ground squirrel, danger was everywhere: in all movement, in all sound, and in silence as well.

It was not surprising then that the wolf cub's presence was quickly sensed. With a sharp little squeak and a sudden spring-like action, the squirrel leaped away, spun around and, on his hind legs, faced his foe. He was a burrower, not a climber, and without his burrow he would have to find another hiding place or stand his ground. He looked about. There were no hollow logs, no piles of stones, no mountains of forest debris. The remainder of the dead tree on which the mushrooms grew was too far gone; there was too little left of its substance to provide shelter. No, it was there—in that glade where the sun fell in shafts and painted stripes on the ground—that the mature, life-wise, thirteen-lined ground squirrel must face the immature, clumsy cub. The outcome was by no means certain.

When the rodent cried out and inconveniently leaped away from the spot where he could easily have been taken, the wolf cub, in surprise and confusion, stood up to his full height. Despite himself, as much as he wanted to be a wolf, the best he could do at first was cock his head to one side and whine. He had not faced such determination before, nor had he ever seen so small an animal rear up, face him, and scold so loudly. It was all rather confounding.

The scolding of the ground squirrel, the shrill outpouring of pure rodent invective alerted every animal around. Songbirds resting the while in nearby brush rose full to the sky and were gone. An owl high in a sheltered place turned his head an incredible three hundred degrees and blinked down. If he had cared—and he surely didn't—he would have cheered the wolf on.

Here in the center of a private and very temporary universe, the white wolf cub became the focus of attention. For the first time in his young life he was on trial; his measure would now be taken. Quite suddenly, although the terms of its understanding were somewhat cloudy, the taking of this prey, the killing of this strange little chattering creature became the most important thing in the world.

The animals he had killed before had been easy. His needle-sharp teeth sank quickly to a vital spot in those small bodies and the struggles ended as suddenly as they began. What could be so very different here? The body was small—although apparently made of a kind of spring steel—and a bite was all that was needed. A simple, quick bite with canine tooth penetrating skull, spine or chest cavity. Nothing more than that, certainly.

One characteristic that marks the rodent is the nature of his strange front teeth. Those four curving, gnawing tools grow for as long as the animal is alive. They never stop seeking a complete circle, for they grow in great arcs that will eventually close and cause the animal to puncture and kill itself—stab itself slowly as it were—if hard and resistant substances are not always at hand on which the teeth can be worn down. A gnawing animal, then, must constantly gnaw in order to stay alive. Because of this dominant fact of life, its four front teeth are always honed to a fine cutting edge, always dangerous to young and inexperienced predators.

And so, without regard for tactics that he would one day know and use as a matter of course, the wolf cub moved in on the ground squirrel. Stiff-legged, a little hesitant, somewhat intimidated by the constant flow of invective that was being heaped upon him in such shrill tones, Lobo began his approach. His first fateful mistake was in letting curiosity get the better of his kill-instinct: as Lobo pushed his snout forward to smell his foe, the ground squirrel, not at all interested in the fine distinction between this indignity and a fatal thrust, fastened himself to Lobo's upper lip and felt his teeth meet in the middle. With a yapping shriek, the wolf leaped backward, outraged, shaking his head and striking at his face with his paws. The ground squirrel lost his grip and hit the ground, rolled, righted himself, and again faced his foe on his hind legs, scolding furiously. Before Lobo's convulsive reaction to the initial pain had enabled him to shake the little rodent loose, he had been bitten three more times by jaws that moved with the speed of a sewing machine.

Lobo stood off now and studied the dancing, chattering sprite. He shook his head from time to time, splattering blood in all directions as it flowed freely from the wounds on his lip and muzzle. The white fur there was stained red, as were his front paws, and there were splatterings on his chest and shoulders. He was, indeed, sorely injured, but not as badly as he may have looked to the casual observer. An animal defending itself against a great predator, even the young of great predators, works under one great disadvantage. If, in its self-defense, it injures its foe, it doubles the intensity of the assault it must face. A wolf is never so much a wolf as when injured in pride or body. A killer is never so much a killer as when a game is involved.

Before the ground squirrel's teeth met in Lobo's face, before this gross indignity was heaped upon him, Lobo wanted to kill the squirrel and lay its drooping body before his parents, and then fight for it with his littermates. But now, all splattered with blood, the young wolf knew it was no longer a matter of *wanting*—it was something he *had* to do.

Wary now, alert to the danger inherent here in the foe, Lobo began feinting in the classic manner of the wolf. First he would make a brief, short rush and then suddenly pull up short, leaving the adversary confounded and increasingly less certain of itself. That was his tactic. In, out, in, out, Lobo kept up the pressure. Soon the little squirrel, with a heartbeat and respiration rate very much greater than the wolf's, was fairly lathered into blind fury. Each thrust by the white wolf cub put him off balance, made him adjust and readjust quickly as the wolf withdrew. Never close enough to bite, yet always thrusting, the wolf became a maddening object, not just a frighteningly large one.

Finally, as Lobo made his thrust, the sense and caution of an animal who had already survived one hostile year gave out and the squirrel charged the wolf. Alert now to the teeth of rodents, Lobo sidestepped quickly, turned and brought his great paw down on the squirrel's back. The little animal twisted within his own skin and cruelly lacerated the cub's right front paw, causing more blood to flow.

The two foes quickly resumed their opposing positions, the ground squirrel on his hind legs, dancing to and fro, the wolf cub circling around him, haunch high, forelegs to the ground. Now, however, the cub was forced to stop from time to time to lick his damaged right front paw. During one such hesitant moment, the rodent grasped an opportunity—returning to his four feet, he streaked past the wolf up the rise toward some thicker wood. Although more an animal of open places, without a burrow at hand he sought cover in any form. His victory, after all, could only come in escape; he could not kill the wolf, and thus he sought only the stalemate he had held with life from the day of his birth.

When the rodent turned his back on the cub, however, he had already made his fatal mistake. Even with his injured paw, the cub was fast enough. In two bounds, still awkward and seemingly more frisky than deadly, he overtook the squirrel. With the advantage of coming up from behind his foe, away from those slashing incisors, he quickly closed his teeth, felt the satisfaction of penetrating living flesh, and held a dead squirrel in his teeth by the time they met in the middle. A single well-placed snap had crushed out its life and made the wolf cub the victor. A career was launched there that day.

With blood still flowing from his lip and from his lacerated pads each time he lifted his paw to take another painful step, Lobo limped back up the rise. He reached the small sheltered area where his parents and littermates lay up in the shade. There were no cheering crowds, no voices to call out "well done." There was, though, a look of approval, a kind of silent acceptance. Once again a cub had done what was right, what was expected and necessary if he was to survive. Wolves are not human beings who must run around reassuring each other, thumping each other on the back; these great wild predators do exactly what they have to do, or they die. The fact that they survive at all is their reward.

The white wolf cub stood at the edge of his family group and looked around. The great tan male sat motionless on the higher ground looking down with his yellow eyes. His silver mate lay in the shade, languid, serene, her softer eyes resting on the white cub as well. Three small bundles of coiled springs and intermeshed gears huddled nearby awaiting a signal giving them permission to explode. Screwed down to the ground by an invisible force, they needed only to be set free to spiral upward and outward in all directions and resume the games. Lobo dropped the limp ground squirrel, let it slip from his jaws. He sank back on his haunches and whined softly. Then, there being no apparent objection from either parent, the cubs let loose. At once they were upon the squirrel, over and around Lobo, and were gone into the brush, tearing after each other, lusting for the prize that Lobo had brought home.

Still under the eyes of his parents, Lobo sank full to the ground and began working on his front paw. From time to time he looked up. The eyes of his parents were never off him, not even after he had fallen asleep to relive the chase and the kill.

FOUR

Each day in the life of the cubs brought new adventures, new lessons. Under the unceasing supervision of the silver and tan wolves they slowly developed and began to lose their infant look. Each in turn entered adolescence—in wolves as in humans a time of long limbs, sloppy gait and complex emotions.

A tragedy struck Lobo's family during that first summer, and from it he learned of things that were to become part of his permanent knowledge. It was one of those matters that cannot be understood by a wolf—not in the same sense that humans can understand—but an experience that has built within it so many signals and signs that the animals can react to it and handle it as if they fully understand. It represents one of those areas where instinct and acquired knowledge work so closely together that it is difficult to separate one from the other.

Lurking within the vast pool of American wildlife is a villain whose one joy is destruction, whose one purpose is death. This great evil—this formless, bodiless waster—is known collectively as *rabies,* nature's soiled reincarnation of the devil. It lurks, hides and shifts from one animal to another, bringing death and torture with it from host to host. So far as is known, this nightmare disease can be carried by and transmitted to any mammal, and only mammals can catch it. Tragically, no animal ever survives it—neither wolf, man, squirrel, nor cow has ever lived once the disease has incubated and Negri bodies formed in the brain. After the Civil War, half a century before the era of the Custer Wolf, skunks were the great reservoir for rabies in the Midwest. At other times, in other parts of the land, it has been bats, foxes, and rats. But each time, in each place, the tragedy has been the same, repeating itself over and over again. Any animal, once infected by the furious form, becomes a wild, raging beast attacking anything in sight. Its signs are often slow in coming, but once arrived they are unmistakable and final.

Somehow that summer—through some unknown, undecipherable chain of tragic events—the disease reached the Dakotas in the body of an infected coyote which had perhaps been bitten by another of his kind— or by a skunk, a weasel, or perhaps a rabbit. One day the silver wolf and the tan were working their cubs along a ridge, hoping for a chance at a lone pronghorn separated from its herd by an injured foot. The tan saw the coyote but did not note anything about it to cause concern. Lurking off to the side to avoid direct contact, as the little brush wolf usually does when the great timbers approach, it did not act suspiciously.

Then suddenly, without warning, it was among them, snapping, snarling, lashing out in all directions. Saliva frothed around its mouth, up onto its muzzle, and it shook its head repeatedly from side to side as if to rid itself of a terrible problem. In the body of the tormented coyote there dwelled a devil indeed, a transmitted death millions of years old so successful that those with reason to defeat it can only do so by suicide. Only by killing all mammals, of which man is one, can man be certain he has destroyed the disease.

The adult wolves reacted immediately. First they gave the warning sounds, the most urgent ones, calling the cubs to their sides. The mane stood up on the tan's neck as he circled warily, trying to keep the snarling coyote away from his young.

Deep in the eyes of the coyote there was great pain. The twitching of his head and neck, the spastic movements that marked his every effort, signaled that the end was near. Tormented now for days by the increasing pain induced by sound and light, driven to near

panic by so much as the twittering of a bird, even by
the sounds of an insect, tortured by the fear of stran-
gling, driven mad by thirst yet afraid to drink, the
pitiful animal was forced to act out this one last cha-
rade in the hydrophobia death-play. Somehow he got
past the male long enough to sink his convulsively
chopping fangs into the flanks of the two badly frightened females in the litter. His infected saliva ran into
the wounds opened by his sharp canines and thereby
condemned both cubs to suffer the same horrible death.

Furious, the male wolf drove again and again at the
mad coyote, trying to avoid contact and yet determined
to drive it away. Finally, exhausted, the coyote backed
off, whining, and slipped into a draw, there to col-
lapse—paralyzed, tormented, near death. During the
ensuing night, after the warmth had left the air and the
chill had set in, there would be no heat left in the
coyote's body to counter it. When morning came, the
body would be stiff, the eyes permanently open, and
rabies would have claimed yet another victim. Deep in
the brain tissue of this hapless animal the incubated
virus would slowly die, content that a life's work had
been done.

In the days that followed, the two infected cubs appeared to be in perfect health. The wounds healed un-
eventfully and there was no sign that either had had a
particularly notable misadventure. But along about the
twentieth day, the smaller female—tan like her father
—began to act in a strange manner. First she would not

eat, and then—during the heat of a particularly hot day, when the family had gathered by a small pond to drink and rest up—she held back. When summoned to the water by the mother's calls, she began to whine, then yap; she ended up by snarling and slinking away. In the hours and days that followed she kept more to herself, falling behind repeatedly, not eating or drinking. On the third day she was abandoned, and almost at once the symptoms began in the other female cub. In three more days she too was left behind; the family of six had become one of four and the silver and tan wolves moved on slowly toward the north, taking their two male cubs with them. The two abandoned cubs slipped agonizingly through the stages of their disease and dissolved unheralded back into the land. It was as though they never had been.

By the time the wolf family had established their new hunting range the summer was full upon the land. It was a good summer; there was rain, and the sun was high but not always burning. The evenings were crisp and clear and the land produced well. Litters were large, foliage ample and grazing good. The browsers and grazers alike flourished and the predators were at peace. Great predators, finding plenty on home ranges, did not shift from range to range; they did not have to migrate across land claimed by others, and therefore fights were few in number and when they did occur, comparatively mild. It was a good, rich time and the cubs learned rapidly what, when, and how to hunt.

Once or twice during this period the wolf family came within sight or sound of human beings. Each time tribal memory came to their rescue and they moved off, anxious and happy to avoid contact. Each time the urgent warning sounds were made and the four wolves slipped away unseen, unrecorded. On occasion their tracks were spotted and some word was passed around that they should be trapped, but nothing was done.

Without realizing what they had done, the wolf family had established their range on the winter pasture of a large and prosperous ranch. It was land that would not be used for several more months and therefore land on which direct encounter with man would be unlikely. Domestic animals were not herded here during the summer months and thus were not generally encountered. There was plenty of food to be had from local fauna and, at least for a time, trouble remained an unfulfilled possibility.

It was not always to be that way, however. When the fall came and a small herd of great red, white-faced Herefords were moved onto the back pastureland, the ancient conflict between man and wolf would begin anew. The wolf's intelligence, remarkable as it is, apparently falls short of being able to comprehend this fact: that the taking of domestic stock is like the signing of a death warrant. Wolves often take domestic stock even when it is unnecessary, perhaps because these great fat creatures—whether pigs, sheep, or cows—are virtually crippled by domestication and are the easiest of all prey. But the lazy wolf who takes this course of easy living is inviting an unparalleled wrath upon not only his own head but the head of every wolf in the land.

Moreover, the human settlers in this area—the Dakotas, Nebraska, Wyoming—are almost to a man descended from one of the cultures of Europe. Whether from England or Ireland, France, Germany, Spain, Sweden, Norway, Denmark, Russia, or Italy, they or their forebears brought with them a hatred of the wolf. To them, the wolf had been the legendary embodiment of evil since before the dawn of history in Europe. With paintings hung on their walls of mad, snarling wolves attacking sleds being drawn across the snow by a brace of terrified horses, or with legends suspended in the dark recesses of their minds testifying to werewolves and the like, little wonder that these immigrants from Europe so despised the wolf. To them, the one good thing about the animal was the status he gave to the man who killed him—no matter how easy the killing may have been.

On the other hand, the Indians who belonged to this land, who were here first, did not feel this hate. Rather, they honored and respected this great predator and named clans and warriors for him. Far to the east, on the shores of the great Atlantic Ocean, Natick Indians had known this animal as *mukquoshim, mummugquoshum,* or sometimes simply as *mogke-oaas,* the "great animal." Although the wolf had disappeared from southern New England by 1850 (an intrepid hunter killed the last Connecticut wolf on the outskirts of Bridgeport in 1837), *mogke-oaas* lived on in the memory of all who knew the stories of the Indians, who in turn had known the wolf. Here the wolf of legend had long outlived the wolf of fact.

Across a broad continent, in southeastern Alaska, the few thousand or so Tsimshian Indians still surviving the whiskey, firearms, smallpox and measles of the white man could still send their representatives to a council fire there to hear it intoned, *Lelyitxal keboal aL laxamauksal aL saXL Ksan. NLke wool kebol txanetkSL SEM-gigadEm wan.* Literally translated into the alien and unrhythmic English tongue, the story begins: *They had a feast the wolves on a prairie at the mouth of Skeena River. Then invited the wolves all the chief deer.* In this tale the clever wolves forced the deer to laugh. The deer in so doing revealed the inferior quality of their teeth and were slain and devoured. The story accounts for the deer's dread of the wolf.

The same people told of a little wolf who came upon a human hunter abroad in desperation trying to find food for his starving people. The little wolf gave explicit instructions which were followed to the letter by the frantic man, and soon he became rich from the grizzly bears he was able to kill and sell. Only when he lent the little wolf, who was trussed up in a skin bag, to a friend who did not follow instructions did the wolf's magic fail. Other wolves in legend have helped the Indian catch the salmon, outsmart birds and generally master the world.

Far to the south, in southeastern Arizona, the Pima Indians told of the wolf *Rsu-u-u* who joined forces with the puma *Mavit*. One day, for reasons not entirely clear, the wolf decided to summon his cousin the coyote. ("Cousin" is a fair evaluation of the relationship the coyote actually has with the timber wolf in the scientific definitions of the white man.) With great insight and understanding the wolf took the kidney of a deer and roasted it, allowing the wind to carry the odor far. The coyote got the scent, understood the message, and came to join his kin. When it was found that the coyote was nearly dead from starvation because he could not retain his food, the wolf found and repaired a rip in his hide through which the food was escaping, and the coyote thrived.

North again, in Alaska, the Tlingit Indians in their Na-dene language called many chiefs of many fine houses by the name of wolf; in the Star House (*Qotxanaxa*) the chief was called *Yakwan*, Swimming Wolf. In *Tcak kudi*, Eagle's-nest House, the chief was *L!ex* or Gray Wolf; in *Tcal*, or Halibut House, the chief was *Datxiagutc*, which meant Wolf Walking Around a Person. A vague reference to the wolf appears in the name of *Kaknuk*, the traditional chief of *Hinka* (House on the Water). Others were *Datlketsate* (Stomach of a Wolf); *Yanaxnawu* (Swimming Wolf); *Stuwaqa* (Named from a Wolf); *Andeci* (Many Wolves Howling About the Town); *Q!aleq* (Red-mouthed Wolf); *Saxa* (Named from a Wolf's Cry); and *Yandjiyitgax*

(Hungry Wolf Crying for Food). To these peoples the wolf was the embodiment of many desirable traits—skill, craft, understanding, inventiveness, strength, courage. Thousands of children were named for the admired predator.

In another Indian legend from the northwest, *Txamsen* (the raven) comes to know that well-fed wolves are friendly, even hospitable animals that need not be feared. In the state of Washington the Bellabella Indians knew of *Ts!emkalaqs*, the woman who had four children by a wolf. One of her sons, *Iaxis*, had a very eventful life as a canoe-builder and painter of stones. When he died he became the devilfish. To the Nootka people it was *L!eHmamit* (Woodpecker), chief among the wolves, who alone in the original world had the secret of fire. Elsewhere on the vast continent the wolf figured with equal prominence in legend, in song, in sacred names, even in actual religion.

When the tan wolf and his silver mate and their two cubs took up hunting on the edge of a cattle ranch, they did not have Indians to contend with. Their adversaries were men with paler skins and a paler understanding of the ways of this land.

There was an expectancy of error that condemned the wolf before he had sinned. Man, eternally guilty of crimes beyond counting—man the killer, the slayer, the luster-for-blood—has always sought to expurgate himself of his sin and guilt by condemning the predatory animals. Whenever outraged, ever-righteous man kills a wolf, he therefore symbolically punishes the predator in himself, and stands cleansed by his deed. This strange recurrent theme must be noted as a product of civilization. The more "civilized" man becomes the less he can tolerate himself and the more important the death of the wolf seems to be.

FIVE

I T was late summer, a hot day on the plains, and the
light was yolk-yellow. High above the world of the
wolf a layer of mist stolen from a distant ocean surface
by a hot sun drifted aimlessly, waiting for the winds to
tell it what to do. The mist took the light of the sun,
bent it, twisted it, and made it different. Thousands of
feet below this layer of vapor another drifted, more
sullen, newer to the sky. A layer of fine dust—sand
ripped from the earth by a recent wind that had raped
a desert—had blinded a toad and taken the crest from a
casually drifting dune and sent it aloft, whistling,
stinging, tumbling, abandoned. High up it had spread
out, fine particles floating only because they were too

light to do anything else. There these yellow mites of wasted earth took the newly water-scattered fragments of sunlight and contrived new tricks, new interpolations of bounce-and-reflect, so that when the light finally fell to earth ninety-three million miles from the point of origin its once white light was like the heart of an egg. This strange light bathed the earth and gave a haunted cast to the commonplace, drenched the known with the mood of the unknown.

Through this vaporous yolk the wolf family moved. Across the open, flat land they hunted: the great tan male, the silver she-wolf and the two partially grown male cubs—all that remained of the five born in the litter. Moving about a half a mile ahead of the others, the male constantly scanned the horizon, scouted in the air, tasted the wind. He was alert to two distinct phenomena, one being prey, which he could kill, and the other man, who could kill him. Since taking up their new range on the pasture land of a large and prosperous cattle ranch, they had encountered the man-smell often. Each time the strange odor lifted off an object, or drifted up from the ground, the tan wolf growled softly. Even if he could have spoken, in the sense that men speak, he could not have related the incident of the black wolf—the day of the guns and his own grievous wound. But he had a kind of memory of it after the fashion of the wolf; it had burned itself into his conscience, as surely as the bullet had burned its way into the flesh of his flank and had become a part of his special learning. It would always elicit the same response.

The index system of scents among wolves is perfect and lifelong. Each smell has an association that is immediately recallable. Stimulation and response are but a fraction of a second apart, reaction time too short to measure.

The female was no less alert, no less attuned to the world, its treasures and dangers, its odor-induced memories both good and bad. Even the cubs had built up a reasonable file in their one spring, their one summer. Not every smell was new now, nor was every aroma a blank stimulus. They recognized the distinctive scents of many creatures; they knew rain while it still lay in the womb of the sky; they knew accumulated water in a pond or a spring at a great distance.

The wolf is keyed to his world not only by his nose: his eyes and his ears, too, know the measure of his experience, the needs of his survival. No animal taller than the grass itself can move within a mile and not be seen, and anything much taller can be seen at far greater distances. A creature on the move whose back and ears do not protrude above the cover of prairie vegetation can be spotted at remarkable distances, for the grass and weeds moving with him stand out from the velvet-constant surroundings. Without movement, however, any animal silhouetted against the sky can be safe; a bison or a steer is as much a tree as a tree itself unless there be sound, odor, or movement—or perhaps the stimulation of another sense we do not know.

A wolf, it has been said, can hear a cloud pass overhead, and perhaps there is truth in that poetic figure.

For in dealing with so remarkable a creature, who knows tomorrow's established fact from today's apparent hyperbole? The hearing of a wolf is keen beyond belief. Among the uncounted sounds that descend on him each day, the wolf is able to extract those that have meaning, those that have value, and in an instant's time he can extract those values and meanings and react. A bird's cry can be interpreted, a movement in the softest vegetation can be read like a book, even the stomach rumblings of a ruminant can be used like radar. Nothing escapes this sense, not even silence itself.

Thus, as the male moved ahead of his family, all three of his distance senses were working in consort—scanning, probing, searching. It may be that still other senses were at work as well, for the Indians who have known the animal longer and better than we have (and who know special things about the natural world that we cannot know) swear it is so. In their stories, and in the stories and symbology of other peoples close to the land, they have given the wolf special powers, acknowledged him to be superior in many private ways. And who can deny this?

Whatever his powers, the tan was using them that yolk-yellow day, for the wind carried a strange sensation with it. It could be heard, but it could not be felt; it could be sensed, yet the grass did not move. It was a day as much mood as reality; it was a lazy day, yet full of foreboding. In the distance a signal was sent. Whether it was received by the wolf first as a sound, a sight, or a smell we cannot know, but received it was, and he froze as he stood and slowly sank toward the ground. The rough hair along the ridge of his spine and the great mass of it around his neck and shoulders bristled, moved forward and up. His ears snapped forward, grasping for a mere fraction of a sound. The she-wolf and the two cubs saw the change in the tan's attitude, read the signals and followed his example. High overhead a hawk, painted yellow by the weird light, skidded in his lazy arcing, changed his course, and watched intently from his reduced circles. Action was promised below and what might follow could so disturb the surroundings that small rodents and sleeping birds would expose themselves and be easy for the taking.

In fact, a hunting wolf, a large predator tuned to the kill in any land, is an electric force that automatically signals a waiting, somnambulant world. Small prey animals move off quietly, happy to be overlooked, but are often preyed upon by smaller killers, alerted by their movement. The clean-up squadrons—the buzzards, condors, or vultures, and the ravens and crows, the jackals, hyenas, or coyotes, depending on where you are—all get the message and interpret the signals: a kill is in the offing . . . a kill is in the offing . . . a kill is in the offing. This, the world's first telegraph, works without wires and has no fuses to blow.

And so the tan lay watching, waiting for newer and more definitive signals. Suddenly the smell was there—a passenger on an innocently shifting wind—the dank, steamy smell of a cow and her bawling calf. The two unsuspecting animals were moving across the wolves' front, coming up slowly out of a draw less than half a mile ahead, emerging like offerings from the soil itself. In an instant they were in full silhouette, large and meaty in profile before the hungry predators, ripe and ready for the plucking.

No language was necessary; everything that need be said about the situation had long ago been discussed by the forebears to these wolves. Swiftly analyzing the direction of travel of the Hereford and her calf, the she-wolf swung off in the same direction at a trot, her tail streaming behind, bush full and indicative of her now happy mood. The male skulked low in the opposite direction; then, satisfied that he was free of his intended prey's peripheral vision, he struck out at a run to bring himself directly behind the cow, which was alert now only to a wolf and two cubs running a parallel course.

It was several minutes before the cow's dull senses could understand that the wolf running neck and neck with her was coming closer with each step, angling in toward her. Their paths were no longer parallel, but converging. Each time the great beast brought her front feet to earth a great thudding, belching sound came forth. Able to move quickly if need be, but not prepared for long races, the cow would soon be winded, would soon haul up, and as her calf skidded to a bawling stop against her, would turn in confusion and try to face four dancing, prancing wolves at once. No less in love with life than a wolf, she would attempt to fight, would keep her head low hoping to hook a wolf and throw it, hoping to have a carcass to worry and hoof into the dirt. The male calf would only bawl, keeping up the lament that started with his birth and would not stop until his short life was ended.

It was, indeed, soon over and the wolf family stood panting over the two prostrate forms. As dusk fell, the air cooled and the world of day came to a halt, relinquishing the land and the sky to the world of the night. From one into the other the wolf family feasted. They took great quantities of fresh meat, because their position was too exposed and they must withdraw before morning, find a secluded spot and lay up through the heat of the next day. Had they made their kill in a sheltered area, as in the draw from which the stray Hereford cow and her calf had come, they would have remained near the carcasses and fed several times more, as long as there was anything edible left. But in the time of Lobo, on the great flatlands of the American West, the pressure was already on and wolves, in the interest of self-preservation, were forced to become something they had never been before: wasteful.

Before dawn streaked the sky, feeling out another yellow day, the wolves were gone. They had moved off across a ridge, a full ten miles from their kills, and had denned up in a rocky area that gave them a commanding view of all approaches. Here had once stood a mighty mountain range, and here the forces of water, wind, winter cold and searing summer heat had conspired to wear it all away, nibbling the soaring masses down and feeding its mineral chips and dissolved chemicals to the land. This chipping and wearing had gone on for millions of years, and excluded only a small tumble of rocks harder than the rest, more durable than most. In this tumble of time-resistant boulders the wolves hid after their crimes had been committed. Thus did nature, over a span of millions of years, create the wolf-den site even before she had created her first wolf. She may have loaned it to an aggressive dinosaur and leased it to a saber-toothed tiger somewhere along the way.

Shortly after the wolves had abandoned what was left of their double kill, several coyotes moved in and began to dismember the bones that remained joined. There was a short tussle at daybreak when a bitch coyote and a badger that had moved in had an argument over a piece of hide. By the time the sun was well up birds were perched on the offal, buzzards to the number of ten, and several ravens. Others arrived with each passing minute. Unseen but perhaps more efficient than any other members of the clean-up squads were the insects that worked from below, entering crevices where the backboned animals could not go, attending to carrion details ignored by those with larger appetites.

The day was hot, with a sun burning full down for its length, and by afternoon the bones had begun to bleach. Toward nightfall thunderheads began to build up overhead and rain was promised. Unknown to the wolves, who had now moved out of their rocky retreat and were moving under cover of night back toward their own den site ten miles distant, and unknown as well to the rancher and his hands seeking several head of cattle that had strayed during the preceding days, a race was mounted against fortune, good and bad. The wolves had left tracks, clear tracks that could not be confused with a coyote's dainty tread. A wolf cub will have feet broader than those of an adult coyote, even though the coyote may be larger in overall size; there can be no confusion between the two.

Those wolf tracks, set into the dust that lay upon the dry, late-summer land, would wash away with the first rain and be gone forever, carrying with them the story of what had happened during that yellow day. It was a race between the storm building in the sky and the sun crawling across other lands, edging out the night in Pennsylvania, Ohio, Indiana, and Illinois, infringing upon South Dakota. With that sun, riders from ranch house and bunk house would come across the bones. If the rain came first, they would say "coyote" and curse, and maybe shoot a skulking animal or two in vengeance. If the rain held off until the riders arrived, they would see the tracks and the wolves now moving away from the area for a few weeks to hunt elsewhere would find a full-scale war awaiting them once their cyclic pattern had brought them inevitably back to the same flat land.

The rider from the ranch knelt beside the skull of the cow, turned it over with his gloved hand, looked up as thunder crashed overhead. Rising to his feet he cast about like a good hound, and as the first rain drops pocked the dust he went again to his knees and spread his hand flat on the ground palm down next to a full, clear track left by the great tan. He looked up, and as the now falling rain cut furrows in the dust on his face, he screwed his eyes against the elements, whistled quietly, and said to his companion nearby: "Wolf. And a big 'un." His estimate of size was lost as a bolt of chain lightning cleaved and the thunder struck with an awesome crash.

But the word had been spoken and a thousand years of hate—an embodied resentment against an animal that was more a fictionalized symbol of destruction than an agent of it—flowed as free as the falling rain. The word "wolf" had been spoken and its echo, clanging back toward the ranch house, would beat plowshares into swords. War was declared.

S I X

THE order of battle was quickly drawn. The plan was determined, the logistics arranged for, and the troops put into motion. A trap was needed, made from steel processed in Detroit from iron ore mined on Michigan's Upper Peninsula, using coal from Pennsylvania laid down as muck when the wolves' ancestor was the size of a horse. Fabrics would be used made of cotton grown in Georgia, woven in South Carolina, processed in New York. Instructions were obtained from the Federal Government in the District of Columbia on the Potomac, printed on paper manufactured in New Jersey from wood grown in Maine, with ink produced in Connecticut by workmen from Germany. Dozens, perhaps hundreds of men represented by innumerable labor unions had joined together to produce in fraternal love and brotherhood the tools required by one man to kill one wolf. The wolf's forces were somewhat more modest—he had, in fact, only himself, and the desire to live.

The actual work involved in the trapping was elaborate and ritualistic. The tan wolf, in moving through the flat country, had, in good wolf practice, established scent posts. At specific places, at fairly uniform distances, he had urinated on upright objects, thus marking his hunting range and informing any would-be intruders that a claim had been staked. There were bushes, some range grass stubble, and an old bleached-out carcass, dead from other causes, included in this array of markers.

The trapper's first task was to locate such a post, readily identified in dry weather by toenail scratches where the wolf had dug after voiding. The rain had washed such easy signs away, but a likely scent post was selected for the first trap set. As luck and the trappers would have it, the choice was a wise one.

Once the site was selected great pains were taken to prepare the trap. First, a wolf that had been captured as a cub and held prisoner in a small, cruel crate for just this purpose was killed with a blow from an ax. His gall was collected, along with his anal glands—fatty, bluish lumps from either side of his vent. This frightful mess was added to a bottle of urine previously collected and the whole allowed to sit for several days with an ounce of glycerine added to give it body and a grain or two of corrosive sublimate as a preservative. A few drops of this incredible witch's brew was then rubbed on the soles of the trapper's boots and on the fingers of his gloves. These articles of clothing had previously been "cured" in a steamy pile of manure behind a barn.

From the manure pile, too, had been taken a piece of cotton cloth about three feet square, a small piece of circular screening three inches in diameter, and the steel trap itself. A steel post about two feet long, a heavy wooden paddle, and a six-foot length of heavy iron chain were the last treasures retrieved from the manure before the task was begun.

Near the scent post, the drop cloth, richly aromatic from its sleep in the manure pile, was spread and on it the trapper knelt. With his equally savory paddle he excavated a hole in the dust about twenty inches across and six inches deep. The same paddle was used to pound the sharpened stake deep into the earth beneath the dust, giving it firm purchase against the frantic tugging it would know if the trapper was successful. Carefully, the gaping trap was set into the hole, the area beneath its pan religiously cleansed, leaving no pebble to mar its function or jam its springs. The trap pad, cut from an old window screen, was carefully placed over the trap's pan and the dirt collected on the drop cloth was moved back over the trap, burying it about a half inch below the surface. The stake and chain were similarly covered and the excess dirt carried far away for dumping. A small piece of brush was placed back at the edge of the trap site and the brew—the bubbling black brew missing only tongues of toads and eyes of vampires—was sprinkled about, enriching the scene with its unique fragrance. The trap, as set and left to welcome the wolf, was invisible, and just a little lower than the surrounding land. There was a good reason for that very slight difference in altitude. Stepping into a slight depression, even a very slight one, would cause the wolf to step harder. Not only would the trap be more certain to spring, but the bite would be farther up the wolf's leg, surer, truer, more professional.

As a final gesture, a kind of salute to him who was about to die, a second brew was used, one constantly in preparation, ever ready for wolf or coyote. A milk can half filled with coarsely ground carp and catfish had been left standing in the sun for thirty days. A vent was left open (because a government brochure had warned that there was the danger of an explosion unless the accumulating gases were allowed to escape) and a screen placed over it (because a benevolent government had also cautioned that flies would lay their eggs in the filthy mess, and maggots would rob the stew of its unbelievable reeking odor). This second scent was ladled off the tortured can and sprinkled in the general area of the trap, hopefully drawing the wolf toward the center; there he would be further intrigued by the mash made from his lamented kin and thus lured to place his foot in the fateful spot.

Actually, one scent would have been enough—but the

hunter was anxious. The ears of the wolf would bring a bounty, as would those taken from the slaughtered prisoner. A dutiful wife would practice a special skill and, by taking certain pieces of the wolf's hide, would create with thread and dexterous needle some very real looking ears that would be identified as coming from yet other wolves, animals that did not exist. All this bounty money was available to anyone with the stomach for the work. It still is.

The wolf family was not long in coming upon the set. It had been expertly placed on their run, a regular trail about one hundred miles in length that carried them across their range and back at regular intervals.

The first time the tan male caught the fish scent he growled a warning that brought his family up short. Carefully casting about, he found a place where some of the noxious substance had fallen on a clump of stubble and carefully examined the spot. Finding nothing to disturb him, he proceeded on to the next spot, drawn in toward the center of a circle by an aroma that clung to his nostrils and refused to release him from its enchantment. He stopped once to roll on a bush that had been sprinkled and continued on toward the center. His family followed at a discreet distance.

About ten feet from where the jaws of the trap lay hidden, the tan caught the full rich blast of the second scent and stopped to examine it as he had the first. Again casting around, he found a focal point of reeking intensity where some had fallen to earth and, once again finding nothing to disturb him, followed its heady richness toward a small piece of brush. As he came upon it he recognized his own scent post, now wonderfully enriched, and prepared to wet it once again, so as to mark a boundary he wanted to remain. It was then, as he maneuvered to his task, that his left hind foot fell into place in the center of the depression.

At once the great tan male leaped forward with a snarl filling his throat and curling his lips. For six terrified feet he traveled before he was thrown violently on his back by the stake and chain which now marked the last measure of freedom he would ever know. The searing pain tore up his leg and ran rampant through his thigh. His foot was immediately numb, for the cruel teeth of the trap had severed a main nerve and sunk deep into the bone of his leg.

The sounds made by the male in the extreme of his anger and agony electrified the she-wolf and paralyzed the cubs with fear. They huddled whimpering at their mother's side as she rocked in indecision, torn by the desire to be with her mate, to help him if possible, and by the absolute demand that she get her cubs away as quickly as possible. Finally, the silver female moved away from the scene of the tragedy, looking back repeatedly toward where her mate lay writhing on the ground, snapping at his leg and tugging vainly at the chain.

All legends to the contrary, a wolf's howl does not normally carry much over a half mile. That night the female wolf's lament carried the full mile to where the

male lay chewing on his leg in an effort to amputate it
before dawn. He stopped only once to answer her, and
so obvious was his pathos, so sad his quavering, that the
trapper looked up from his beans as he squatted by the
fire in the draw and said to his companions, "I reckon
we got him."

When morning came over the feverish land, the men
rode across the range toward the trap site. A well-aped
Indian war whoop announced their victory as they rode
round and round the wolf, jabbing their responsive
horses into a canter. The tan, exhausted from pain and
loss of blood, had chewed halfway through his own leg
in a last desperate bid for freedom. Despite his extreme
condition he kept turning to face his tormentors, his
lips rolled back and a growl, bowel deep, issuing in a
steady stream.

Lunge as he would, no matter the pain it caused, the
tan could not reach the men; nor, spin as he would, was
there any way he could face three men at once. Finally
he sank to the ground, panting, barely able to move.
Two ropes whistled through the air, slicing the morning
ground mist and finding their mark with professional
ease and skill. Although he tried to struggle free, the
ropes slipped easily over his head and tightened cruelly
around his neck. Jerked in two directions at once, he
was unable to turn and reach his own hindquarters
where the third man, the trapper, stood. Now, with the
dexterous ease of the butcher, the trapper leaned forward and severed the tan's leg where he had himself
been at work. Then, wiping the blood from his blade on

the haunch of the snarling, half-strangled wolf, the trapper sheathed his knife and walked to his horse.

This was his gesture of defiance. As the trapper rode off toward the ranch at a fast trot, his companions rode after him, several yards apart, the ropes that trailed behind them forming a wide-mouthed V with a half-mad, half-dead wolf at the point. The tan was dragged brutally through the brush, over the rocks, across the land. Never able to regain his feet, he was mercifully dead by the time his triumphant captors reached the ranch. Without ears, the mangled, tattered body of the once proud animal was draped unceremoniously across a fence, where it drew flies by the hundreds and angry, nervous snorts from every passing bovine. Thus was the vanquished saluted.

The following night, in defiance of all good wolf sense, the silver female led her cubs to the trap site and with her sensitive smell reconstructed as best she could the day's unhappy events. Again in defiance of everything she knew by instinct and lesson she followed the course over which the body of her mate had been dragged until she was within sight and smell of the ranch buildings. Commanding her cubs to remain behind near a great tree, she edged forward and passed between the barn and ranch house. To a chorus of screaming, yapping dogs she bounded across a patch of yellow light pouring through an unshaded window and made it safely to the fence where her mate hung limp and drained. Swiftly she dragged his carcass off into the dark and managed to get it back to where the cubs lay up waiting in their obedience. Whining, the cubs pawed at their father, nuzzling him, trying to gain some simple response. Calling the cubs away finally, the she-wolf led them in a wide circle several times around the main ranch buildings, all the while to the chorus of the yapping dogs. Her last point was again the carcass of the great tan wolf, and by the time the two male cubs were again pressing their dead father, calling for him to love back, their noses were so full of the scent of manure, farm yards, dogs, and man, that they would never forget.

The twice-widowed silver female would manage to raise her cubs to the point where they could care for themselves. And their hatred of man, of his scent and of the scent of his domestic stock, would remain with them for as long as they lived.

SEVEN

NATURE makes the sexes of her children different, gives each capabilities, each special talents. Among some animals the death of one parent means a quick death for the young; among wolves, animals of an uncertain lot, the specialization in many ways is less fixed, the talents of both sexes more flexible. The silver she-wolf was capable of seeing her cubs into their independence. She could teach them what they had to know, she could feed them when their talents were not quick enough to keep their own bodies fueled. Strangely, even when her male cubs reached an age where they could assert themselves, her muzzle would never feel the male-dominant bite; she would never go to her haunches

whining with the exquisite agony of a conquered female—not from her own male cubs, not while she still
reigned as the head of the family unit.

In the months that followed, other wolves would drift
in and out of their lives. A half-grown male, too young
to earn the admiration of the silver female and too old
to require her care, came into their lives for a few days,
vacillated between being a male seeking a mate and an
orphaned cub, could not fit in, and disappeared forever
from their lives. Fascinating on the first day, interest-
ing on the second, slightly annoying on the third, he
was a ghost that came and went, an odor that disappeared into a permanent file but an experience that
would not be remembered. He taught them nothing, and
thus he failed to establish himself in their memories.

On another day, in another part of their range, an
aged female limped soulfully into their lives. She was
beyond the breeding age, no longer of interest to an
unattached male, and obviously widowed, for she had
once been a magnificent animal. Obvious too was the
fact that she was an animal of great skill, a creature in
harmony with her world, for she had survived into
arthritic old age without help. No male hunted with this
old she-wolf, no cubs brought offerings. She had outlived those with whom she had joined, those whom she
herself had created with the magic art of her inner
body. Gray now and very old, yet proud, she appeared
one day—near where the silver she-wolf and her two
cubs feasted on a pronghorn that had been taken only

because old age had come his way as well—and sat
watching at an acceptable distance. Although obviously
half starved and wild to join the feasting, she did not
move toward the kill. The silver she-wolf, meanwhile,
circled the kill several times as her cubs fed, keeping her
eyes always upon the stranger. When her own indecision had passed, the silver female called her cubs away
from the kill; they came only reluctantly, and sat off to
the side, allowing the sad old creature to approach the
carcass, squat painfully, and slowly start to feed. When
she was well into the fresh meat the silver approached
slowly and started to feed again from the other side.
The cubs soon rejoined the two females and fed quietly
in their places. When the silver trotted away from the
kill, her cubs with her, the old female limped along
behind.

The addition of the old female to their family unit
did not unduly affect the cubs, although now there was
sometimes less food than before. Unable to hunt for herself, her gait slow and most uncertain, her teeth broken
and worn, the old hag had asked for and had been
granted care. She was fed for three months without
question or trouble. Then one night she moved off
quietly, rested her great, gray head on her swollen front
paws, closed her clouded yellow eyes and slept; and in
her sleep she slipped easily away and rejoined the legends from which she had once arisen.

Whether she became a figure on a totem pole along
the northwest coast of the continent, whether she be-

came a legendary figure who would find and gently rear human children, or whether she would become the dreaded mankiller whose only pleasure was in the cries of her human victims, mattered little to her. To whichever legend she was assigned, however it was recorded—in skillfully sculpted wood or spoken word alone—she was a wolf that had come and gone, lived and died, and hence was part of a living, self-reproducing legend. In her whole life not one man knew her measure, knew her style. She was a night shadow in life; only in death would the experts among men know her well enough to discuss her. Even at that time of recent history there were men who believed she would return to earth in the body of a man to raid graveyards, or to kill helpless women and children to lap their blood. On nights of the full moon she would resume the lupine form and lust for the forbidden: an anti-Christ incarnated. Such things were thought of this tired old wolf as she lay dying, for she was a wolf and that made all men experts—and made all nonsense believable.

Like all creatures who are to be reincarnated, the old wolf knew of none of this as she approached death and would not have cared had she the power to understand it. The matter was of equally little concern to the silver she-wolf and her two male cubs when they came upon the now cold body of the ancient wolf the following morning. They had no emotions. They stopped, sniffed her body, and moved off toward the new day with its tasks and its dangers.

The land where the silver she-wolf hunted and raised her cubs is open to the Arctic. Lying to the east of the majestic mountains of the West, and to the west of the older and therefore lesser hills of the East, the vast plain stretches away across the vastness of Canada to the land of tundra and permafrost, and then, without interruption, to the fields of ice and eternal chill.

When the permanently bad weather of the far, far North worsens in winter, monstrous winds scream southward, bringing a kind of great paralysis to the open lands to the south. Temperatures measurable at fifty and sixty below zero, with winds in excess of eighty miles an hour, bombard all that lives, while treacherous, drifting snow masses against every upright object. All moisture in the air and on the surface of the ground is sucked into communion with falling temperatures and their stuff is transformed from liquid to solid. The air becomes dry and brittle; because of the moistureless quality of all matter and substance, any movement causes an actual crackling sound. Cold is no longer felt as cold but rather as brutal, numbing, shocking pain. Chill is replaced with a frame-wracking ache as the cold penetrates the body and battles with heat-producing and heat-regulating mechanisms for possession of the host. Death can be instantaneous, as eternal as death from any other cause. When Arctic conditions grip the land, when the moisture has been snatched from the air, ice particles become suspended and the sun's oblique rays are refracted. It is a time when you can "hear" the

light, a time of tinkle and chime, when a breath is a
whistle, when movement is pain—and when hunger is so
deep as to seem a part of life itself, not just an instinctive urge to preserve it. This is the time of extreme
danger for the wolf, for his stamina is at a low ebb and
even the slightest exertion forces him to pant, causing
the frozen air to sweep into his lungs. The wolf's feet,
too, are in danger at such times. Ice and snow become
knife-edged and small ridges slice rather than give way
beneath his weight. Cut pads mean loss of blood and
reduced speed; even pain itself can be debilitating.

Through such bad times the silver she-wolf was
forced to lead her rapidly maturing cubs. Like three
ghosts, the silver one, the white one and the tan one
moved, slipping soundlessly from one frozen mist patch
to another. With muscles aching, with feet cut and fur
frosted and rimed, the three sore and tried creatures
hunted a land that rejected them. A paw so sore that
the mere flexing of it was a living agony worked list-
lessly at a frozen spot of ground. Even when nails were
loosened, the ground was scratched—perhaps an incredibly sensitive nose had detected the frozen yet lin-
gering aroma of a dead bird buried beneath a steel-hard
frost. An hour later, in the yellow glare, a sparrow
might be revealed, a mere mite of flesh; without passion,
still in lethargy, the frozen bit would be consumed, an
ice block of carrion crushed apart into slivers pulled
stomachward by a convulsive swallowing, there to sit
frozen for many minutes before beginning to thaw.

The dryness of the air also caused great thirst, which could be alleviated only by the eating of snow. On many days, when the wind was too high, when a nose however keen could help little or not at all, the three wolves would bed down but a few yards apart and allow the drifting snow to cover them. With surprising effectiveness their fur, aided by the layer of crystalline flakes, would hold in their body heat, so that it was warmer under the snow by far than in the exposed places open to the wind.

The relationship of cubs to mother was a changing thing. Her body had ceased to produce milk for them and they no longer bedded down in her embrace. Only when bred again would the chemical changes occur within her that would cause glands to swell and enrichen; only then would part of the food she consumed be diverted to the task of supplying the minerals necessary if she was to feed others. Unbred for that winter, she was dry and there was nothing in her for the cubs except her skill at killing. By this means alone could she feed them.

Often, after days without food, with their guts aching and their tempers short, the family of three would bed down and wait the passing of a storm. In the kind of super-irony that only life itself can provide, they often bedded down within inches of living flesh. In places underground, in dens hollow and lined, the vast rodent population of the plains slept away the bad times in the magic sleep of hibernation. Those that had survived their natural enemies—the wolf and coyote, the eagle, hawk, weasel and snake—had become fat and sassy toward the end of the summer and had disappeared underground with the first chill warnings. Those first Arctic harbingers had forewarned them that a new pattern of instinctive behavior was called for; soon the empty dens had filled and the thriving prairies had emptied. Beneath ground, free from harm or want, they rolled in fatty sleep, their heartbeat and respiration rate all but stopped completely, their body temperature almost as frozen as the air above. More dead than alive, they neither knew nor cared about the plight of the wolf who had no such magic, who was cursed to live through the bad times without recourse. For him, to approach death as closely as the rodents would be a one-way trip.

To the west, the bears had a better solution. They found a rocky cave, a hollow log, a pile of debris—or even excavated their own hole in the ground—and curled up fat and content to approximate the act of the rodent. And so the great bear slept—not in true hibernation, not reduced so far in bodily function, yet quieted further toward death than the wolf could ever know. Warm weather would awaken them, cranky and mean, and cold weather would return them to sleep. Great sows would come awake long enough to help their cubs appear in late January or early February, but even they would go back to sleep.

While so much of the world reposed, the wolves remained awake, and hungry. Their fat stores were soon used up and their hides sat on muscles, their organs touched each other. Since constant replenishing was necessary, any food at all was taken. Other predators, normally overlooked or passed by, were attacked. A coyote was killed when careless enough to come close; mink and weasel were killed in their snarling, twisting fury when found and caught. The smallest speck of flesh or icy carrion was consumed, bone, hair and all. No offal was left, no chance to survive overlooked.

A major kill was cause for wild feasting. Gluttonous appetites were fed, and food was, in the vernacular, wolfed. A kill with parts unconsumed was not abandoned, but the laying up was done nearby until there was nothing at all left, not bone or antler, that could possibly be eaten. Much was inevitably lost to equally desperate meat-eaters without kills of their own.

Somehow the female had skill enough and the winter passed, leaving the family of three intact. When the winds and the chill, the snow, the ice and agony retreated toward the north, pursued by the spring as relentlessly as they had only weeks before pursued every living thing challenging them, the wolves were still alive. Though their coats were bedraggled, their lips, pads and tongues cracked, their eyes bloodshot, their walk slow and uneven, their energy at low ebb, yet they lived. Their beauty and their grace, their flowing speed and rich voices, their wonderful passions, their pulsing love affair with life would return. Spring is more a time of rejoicing because life has survived than for any other reason. Little wonder a song is heard to fill the air, that each day makes you want to cry with joy. Life—*life*—has survived.

And so the three wolves sat hunched on a thawing hill and sang day into night. Their howls grew richer with the hours, and the rime fell away from their fur.

EIGHT

SPRING is a time of change. Great new things come about within the bodies of all that live, plants and animals alike. Those living things that have emotions, however primitive their character, feel the change in that secret part of their world as surely as in their muscles, bones and glands. It is a time for the new, a time for the young—and a time for the old to feel young.

The Arctic agony roared in reverse and whistled itself in diminishing tones back into the refrigerated cauldron of the North. Ice flecked away from tree trunks, noises were heard at the stream's edge and white islands floated away to crash over waterfalls or melt before getting there. Turtles frozen in solid ground, frogs in mud, and snakes rolled in great balls in the guts of a hill, all began to stir. Bats roosting farthest in the cave, those that survived, began to emerge, for the insects were about. Black loam opened a million times in a million places, like so many wombs, and allowed small shoots to thrust toward the sun and the warming winds. Even small patches of snow surviving in shaded places felt the urgency of life from below and parted with due respect for the early plant shoots.

Near the surface of the soil small disturbances began to occur. Earthworms risen from deep below began ingesting soil, passing it through the tubes of their bodies, extracting that which was to them life-giving, and in so doing prepared the soil for new growth and new tasks of richness and fertility. The saliva trails of the worms were, in turn, easily followed by the nearly blind ones, the bizarre, silky moles, who tunneled after in frenzied pursuit, fighting off starvation. No one heard a worm call out, or heard the crunching of the mole's specialized teeth or the satisfied sounds he made, but the agony of death had been there and spring had surely arrived.

A shrew will die in seven hours if not fed, so rapid is his metabolism. They too were abroad to welcome the spring with its offerings of living flesh. Small mice—pink and hairless, blind and deaf—barely had time to squeak once before sharp needles found a fatal spot and all struggles ceased. Like a machine whose sole task was the ingestion of the world, each shrew ate his way across his quarter acre and back, twenty-four hours a day.

Once again sap coursed through the veins of

branches and stems and small green lumps revealed their wonderful secrets and the trees and plants assumed their shapes. Smells arose from the earth, descended from branches swaying overhead, seeped free from every living thing and saturated the world. Since winter can truly be characterized as the time without odor, perhaps it is the odor of spring that is most stimulating; for now, in the land where the wolves walked, there were loam smells, flower smells, and the fragrance of fresh, running water. There were damp smells and warm smells, and the oozing of life smells. The wonderful, warm, oversexed, gravy vapors of spring were upon the land and there was nothing to do but rejoice.

High above spring had also come. Against the blue sky, pocked with fluffy white, new circles were being drawn—the thrilling, living geometry of winged creatures. From the south, from the safety of warmer places, the birds had returned fairly bursting with life potential. They brought the song to the land; they were its voice in the daylight hours, just as the wolves and coyotes were in the dark.

In the early morning hours, when the air was still frosty, the wolves would often lay up in a sheltered spot and listen to the March-to-May symphony of the prairies—the *boom-ah-b-o-o-m, boom-ah-b-o-o-m* of the prairie chickens at their mating grounds. Unobstructed, the sound would carry clear for two miles or more, but without revealing its source. These succulent, two-pound birds would carry out their ancient rituals

in private while singing to the world. Just before dawn
they would gather, as many as fifty at a place, and the
dance would begin. Feather tufts on the males' necks
would stand out like horns, and wings and tails would
drape down, dragging on the ground. With heads low
and necks rigid, the males would rush—first in one direction and then another—inflating the orange sacs on
their breasts, expelling the air suddenly with a violent,
jerky effect that made the characteristic booming
sound. Then again, at other times, they cackled de-
mentedly and rose full into the air, coming to earth
near a rival to whom they gave the same display. Thus
the strange, dream-like tournament would ensue. The
whole wild display—a combination of color, movement,
sound, and instinct ancient and tried—was an ode to
fertility, a testament to life. The sounds of it (and later
the odor of it accidentally come upon) told the wolf of
the plenty that lay ahead. And the olive-green eggs
speckled with brown that followed these displays would
offer further testimony.

On occasion the wolves heard the unmistakable
whirrrrrrrrrr of the rattlesnake's unique tail and
would alter course to avoid contact. Seldom will a wolf
accept the challenge and kill a rattlesnake; more often
the danger is avoided, for by instinct the wolf knows the
nature of the reptile and the damage it can do if disturbed or attacked. The rattlesnake can have no purpose to pursue a wolf, but if threatened it will not hesi-
tate to strike. Fast as a wolf is, he is often not fast
enough. Should an apple fall from a low branch, six

feet from the ground, before the apple lands a rattle-snake can raise the first one third of his body from the ground, pull it back into a loose S, snap forward quicker than the eye can follow, open his mouth until his jaws approximate 180 degrees, swing his two hypodermic fangs down from their protected position in the roof of his mouth, stab his fangs deep into the target flesh, clamp his bottom jaw shut, contract the muscles in his neck—thus squeezing venom from a gland, forcing it forward through the ducts, down through his teeth, deep into the victim—open his jaw, unhook his fangs, curve them back to the roof of his mouth, close his mouth, withdraw from the strike position, lower himself to the ground, and start away. All that before an apple drops six feet. Against such speed, such incredible skill, the wolf was well warned. The cubs jumped convulsively when they heard the sound, the *whirrrrrrrrrr*, and no one can say for certain whether it was a learned reflex or one that arose from instinct. Perhaps both miracles were involved.

Through this world—of *boom-ah-b-o-o-m* and *whirrrrrrrrrr*—the wolves moved, part of it all, the trimmers of surplus, the takers of young. Left alone, allowed to remain a part of a natural setting, the wolves harmed nothing except individual animals; and in this natural world, individuals do not count. What mattered was that spring followed winter and life followed death. Young were born and passions, great and small, produced the next generation, proof that the earth would

never again return to the sterility and barrenness of its
first few million years. Through this the wolves moved
—hunting, finding, belonging—in harmony. It was a
giant cathedral, this spring on the prairies, and the
wolves sang in the choir loft like the rest.

NINE

AT one end of the hunting course followed by the
silver female and her two cubs—near the ranch
that employed the trapper who had taken the great tan
wolf—there was a deep cut, an excavation made
through soft rock by running water. Over a period of
millions of years water had used this course in a runoff
from prairie floods. Originally the ground had been
tilted enough to make the course logical; after the
ground had leveled off somewhat, the cut was deep
enough to draw the free running water to it. Slowly, bit
by bit, minerals had been removed, and finally boulders
tumbled until there existed in the middle of this flat
prairie land a deep gash. Dry most of the year, it could

become a roaring torrent during spring floods. At other times, it was a natural course for animals to follow. During the driest days there would be pools of water in places at the bottom of the ravine, small oases in a desert. Plant life was richer here, too, and shelter existed in a thousand forms, rock tumble, cave, tree hollow, brush and weeds. Birds nested, snakes hibernated, weasels hunted, and an endless natural traffic flowed through this slight feature on the face of the earth.

In the early days of that spring on the prairies the draw had run wild with melting snow. In the confinement of the brief run the river had careened in gyrating eddies and swirls before bursting out at the far end to meander southward across the prairie, eventually to sink underground and disappear, only to ooze upward again in a marsh beside the Mississippi River north of Louisiana. Tumbling through that quick slash in the earth went billions of gallons of water, the one substance without which a prairie is a desert. Minerals were displaced and replaced, the canyon walls were reshaped, and a layer of silt was laid down, smoothed, and made ready for the work of the sun.

When the flood had passed, birds walked on the mud, leaving seeds from plants encountered both near and far mixed with their white droppings and dainty footmarks. Small animals moved about, too, and the stuff of jungles and gardens brushed away from their fur. The great miracle of plant migration, so little understood, occurred here as it did year after year. Seeds carried down with the water and silt, windblown seeds, seeds

carried in crop of bird and gut of mammal, all found
their way to the mudflats at the bottom of the canyon,
and soon a garden flourished. Small animals found their
way down into the cut now that the flood had passed,
and larger animals, hunters large and small, followed
them. By early summer, as it had been by early summer
for thousands of centuries past, a little world complete
unto itself grew up and became a fountain of life, one of
the richest pastures around for the eaters of plants and
flesh alike. To this place the wolves often came, and
never left it hungry. Perhaps a deer on one trip, or
several pheasant on another, always there were rewards
for the passing wolves.

Thunderstorms on the prairies are unlike those any-
where else on earth. Day turns to night, no matter what
the hour, in a matter of minutes. Clouds pile upon each
other, sit on top of each other until they reach from the
ground to the top of the sky. Black and menacing, they
surround an area and pour chill winds inward toward
the center. Then the lightning starts. Distant first, and
silent, it slowly creeps forward until the awesome noise
crashes against the sensitive ear and trees split with
horrendous crashes, sparks flying out as the growth
twists in agony on the ground. In far less time than it
can be told a mighty tree is split neatly in two.

When these mighty storms threaten, cattlemen moving their charges from one place to another try to move
them into sheltered areas where they can be watched.
Cattle, not very intelligent creatures at best, are very
prone to panic; they are quick to adopt mass hysteria

and crash off in all directions, as destructive to self as to anything that gets in their way. Sharp hooves, lowered heads, dead weight thrusting and heaving, pointed horns, all are indifferent to life. Like lightning, a herd of panicked cattle is an elemental force in nature, a force without a true direction, without natural controls, without heart or feeling. It is an outgrowth of blind fear. Just as sound consists of waves moving through air, pushing molecules of invisible gas against each other, and just as no single molecule has a discernible personality, so it is with a cattle stampede. It is terrifying for man and beast alike because it not only destroys, it does so without purpose. It goes nowhere, does no good; it merely thunders and swells—and destroys—terminating only with exhaustion as impersonal as the original energy.

It was on a swing through their regular hunting circuit that the silver she-wolf and her now very large young males came upon the southern end of the cut and took shelter as a very large and violent summer storm built up overhead. Huge lumps piled upon each other in the sky like so many fistfuls of oily rags dropped into a heap. The sun was blotted out and cool winds whistled through the ripening grasses and caused little spirals of sand to rise when bare spots were hit. Everything about the day was ominous, and the three wolves moved halfway up the ravine to escape the coming fury.

The young males were about to leave the female. They were mature enough now to seek life on its own terms and no longer responded willingly to her mes-

sages. There were still things they had to learn, but by
and large they now had to make their own mistakes.
Had their sire lived they would not have hung on as
long as they did; but something about the unattached
female—this beautiful, twice-widowed silver she-wolf—
had held them by her side well into their second year.
Still, her command was becoming less compelling with
each day that passed.

On the day they all moved into the cut, however, on
the day of the big storm, they were still together.
Farmers would remember this day for years and speak
of the lightning-caused fires that would come from those
black clouds to destroy three barns and two farm houses
in that one county alone. The white wolf called Lobo,
soon after to be known as the Custer Wolf, would also
remember it in his special way—and for many other
reasons.

When it first became apparent that a major storm
was building overhead, a band of nearby cattlemen, in
the process of moving some three thousand head of
cattle to reserve pasture land, were near the north end
of the cut. In quick conference it was decided to move
the milling, bawling creatures down into the draw, there
to contain them and, hopefully, to reduce the likelihood
of their being scattered when the storm broke. After the
maneuver had been accomplished, three thousand potentially hysterical animals, weighing up to half a ton
apiece, were herded within a mile of three wolves already bedded down under a fallen tree and some wind-
piled brush. The wolves sensed the presence of the cattle

farther up the draw well enough, and no doubt they intended to make a kill after the storm had passed. But with the winds as wild as they were, and with the dust flying and the temperature dropping, the cattle failed to sense the wolves, although there is little they could have done about it had they been more aware.

When the storm finally broke it was a terrifying display. The thunder rolled across the land in an almost continuous roar and resounded off the walls of the draw. The very earth seemed to act as a drumskin. Lightning, in long, slashing diagonal chains one moment and perfectly vertical the next, worried the earth at split-second intervals for 360 degrees. No matter where you looked—up, down, to any compass point—there was yellow fire streaking the sky, energy without limit or control, screaming earthward, bringing with it a little of the vastness of the universe, a little of the mystery of our own atmosphere, a little of the terror of the truly primeval.

The men who guarded the cattle became more and more concerned. The large beasts, stupid and ineffectual in their fear, their brains bred out of them to make room for filets and ground round, milled and bawled. Calling to each other, pushing against each other, they tried to move out of confinement and were constantly in need of being herded back in. The men were forced to move their horses back and forth, perhaps to kick a steer that was edging away or to call their special call. Like a mob waiting to riot, the huge, dumb beasts moved about, complained, moved about some more.

And then the rain itself started. In blinding, wind-driven sheets it slashed its way across the land and within moments of its beginning drenched everything. The men, having worked their way into slickers while still mounted, lowered their heads, tilting them to allow the brims of their characteristic hats to do as much for them as possible. The wind, gusting furiously, drove the rain into the huddled cattle, hitting their flanks like whips and turning the ground on which they milled into a quagmire. The rain running down their flanks was red with the dry dust that had lingered over the cattle like a cloud before the storm began. The longer it rained, the more the cattle moved and shifted, and the worse the muck became. The riders on their horses, hammered mercilessly by the wind and the rain, turned hopelessly to avoid the direct onslaught.

As terrifying as the wind-driven rain was the electric part of the storm. Cascading down from unmeasured heights, the thunder slammed against the earth, shook rock and hill, causing animals and plants alike to quiver and shake in the fury. Deep in their burrows the rodents of the prairies were safe only momentarily, for the storm exceeded their instinctive preparations and the rain traps underground were not deep enough. In peril of drowning, the prairie dogs rushed to the surface, carrying their drenched and whimpering young with them. In their frantic dash for the dubious safety of the surface, they crawled over and across rattlesnakes and no combat was offered them. Organisms faced with elemental conditions having the power of total destruction somehow learn to put aside all enmities.

The man who owned the cattle stood in the door of his ranch house and looked out across the prairie, counted six flashes of lightning in as many seconds, shook his head and retreated. Concerned for the safety of the men who guarded his stock, as well as for the stock itself, he was helpless. Only a frantic call from a hired hand telling him the pigs were drowning forced him out of his lethargy. Slickered, bent against the wind, he went out to offer whatever help two more hands could give.

In the gully, the thunder overhead had made the cattle even more nervous. They were barely contained now and the men neared exhaustion as they fought to control not only the cattle but their horses and their own tired muscles as well. It was hell in the draw and water was beginning to rise to a point where it would be of more concern underfoot than overhead.

About a mile down the draw the wolf family was huddled under its tree trunk and brush. Not fully protected from the rain, they were at least sheltered from the worst of it. By now their senses were near-paralyzed by the elements and they feared to move without being able to sample the world and know what, if any, threats existed. The driving rain and the wind, mixed with thunder overhead, made hearing all but impossible. The sudden and near-total inundation wiped out all smell, and the gloom plus their own poor vantage point made their sight worthless. They had no means of sampling or testing, so they sat as still as they could with their ears laid back and their coats padded with mud.

Then, quite by chance, quite by ill-fated luck, it happened. By the north end of the draw a single bolt of lightning struck a single tree standing on the rim and the tree exploded violently, pitching down onto the backs of the cattle below. With wild bellowing they started off, swept three riders from their saddles and plunged in total hysteria and panic down the draw. Soon all the cattle, victims of the infectious, rampaging fear, joined the sea of heaving, thundering flesh. No power on earth save massed death itself could stop their momentum. An inexorable force was born and thunder on the earth answered thunder in the heavens.

The wolves' temporary lair beneath the log lay directly in the path of the stampede, but they could not know danger threatened until it was literally on top of them. They could not see, nor smell, nor hear it until the last minute—and then they could feel it, feel the ground tremble and throb beneath them. As it grew more apparent they began to stir and move about, trying to pinpoint a source, determine what if any action was called for on their part. They were too late.

Suddenly there it was. A thousand tons of beef began pouring down on them like a sharp-hooved avalanche and all they had to combat it was speed. Spring-laden, they propelled themselves from their makeshift den and sought a line of retreat. On either side, to their east and west, the lines of frantic cattle had already poured. Only in the middle, directly behind them to the north, the cattle had momentarily jammed again, thwarted by the fallen tree. Quickly, however, the jam broke and those pressing from behind forced those in front over the log, there to roll over and over until flayed to ribbons by the hooves of those who pressed from behind. Very quickly the guts of cow and the blood of bull mixed with the rain in the mucky underfoot.

Flat out in full gait the wolves streaked ahead. Unable to turn right or left, they were forced to dodge a thousand natural obstacles at reckless speeds in poor light. Several times the young white male tripped and barely regained his gait without being trampled underfoot. Behind him the bawling and thundering of the herd pressed hard. Ahead Lobo could see the mouth of the draw, there where the water flowed alluvial fans onto the prairie. And there, at the end of the squeeze, he could see safety beckoning.

As Lobo approached the end of the cut only yards ahead of the herd, he could see the streaks and patches of sunlight on the southern horizon that marked the end of the storm. Although he was fast weakening, he knew he must hold, must keep his lungs and heart pumping, his legs working. Yards were reduced to feet, feet to inches, and then, like a projectile from a gun, the white wolf exploded out of the draw onto the flat open ground of the prairie where he could dodge and escape. Like the sound the cannon sends after its ball, the herd also exploded out into the open after him.

But now the white wolf was in his element and, putting out the last full measure of his strength, he ran obliquely across the front of the herd and was soon out of their range, and out of danger. A few dozen yards off to the side he lay down in the soaking grass, panting furiously, to watch the remainder of the herd pass.

Each mouthful of air that he sucked in burned his throat, made his lungs feel as if they were filling with fire. Slowly he lay back in the grass, a patch of white on the green-black of the drowned prairie, and let his head sink down. Impervious to all sound, numbed and shocked, he slipped off into a deep sleep.

And thus, for the first time in his young life, Lobo slept alone, without parent or littermate to link this moment with his past or his past with his future. He was suspended between life as it had been and life as it could be—so long as he had the skill to mold it after the accepted manner of the wolf.

TEN

SEVERAL hours after the stampede had thundered into history, Lobo awoke from his fitful sleep and stood shakily to survey the prairie. Scattered across thousands of acres of open land drifted a herd of three thousand head of cattle. Each animal had run valuable pounds off its frame, had contributed its own blind might to the violent eruption that had left the draw a no-man's-land. The summer violence had moved away, meandering across a sky that offered no resistance, to worry first one county and then another. It was part of a grand display, a mammoth concerto whose conductor was Thor and whose concertmaster was the devil himself. For hundreds of miles around storm systems arose, erupted, interacted and dispersed only to re-form again. The dead and dying among the animal population of the prairies numbered in the thousands.

In the center of this desolation Lobo stood, legs apart, caught in the radically slanting rays of an early evening sun, white and stark against a black land and a still-glowering sky. Like a ghost he stood, risen from the dead, a white silhouette vignetted against a soiled world of shadowy depths. Completely alone now, he looked out over the land he was soon to rule; for the moment he felt only uncertainty.

Moving slowly—partly because he ached in every bone and fiber of his young body and partly because he knew by instinct that he must not attract attention alone in the open as he was—Lobo moved back toward the draw. Cautiously he moved into the mouth of the silent feature, constantly sampling for sight, sound or smell. It was a dead world, quiet like all death, and not easily understood by one so young. Each step brought him deeper into the midst of chaos. Vegetation lay about in a vast stew whose base broth was muck. The frantic evacuations of the cattle mingled ankle deep with the dead of smaller animals caught in the melee, with flowers, shrubs, and indistinguishable masses that in death did not resemble life nor look like anything that could once have lived.

Scattered here and there in the mud lay the carcasses of heifers and calves that had been caught in the stampede and crushed by twelve thousand hooves. In a few more hours they would start to bloat and the morning's sun would see them close to exploding. The flies had already started to settle. Their buzzing counterpointed the death smell as Lobo moved among the dead like the very symbol of the living. The fact that he had escaped this draw to return to it alive was an arrogance and an irony that he, of course, could not appreciate. His being there had purpose, however, a desperately important purpose, and the evaluation of the exquisiteness of the moment was not part of it.

About three quarters of a mile into the canyon Lobo's progress was suddenly arrested. Without realizing at first just what it was that had caught him up, he suddenly froze. He felt the fur along his back and around his neck ruffle involuntarily. His ears snapped upright and his lips curled back in the most profound snarl the young wolf had ever attempted. Instinctively he lowered his silhouette and began sorting stimuli as fast as they were received, quickly painting a picture, establishing contact with the source of his discomfort.

Ahead of Lobo, not more than a dozen feet away, lay the form of a man, wet, bleeding, exuding the smell that Lobo had been taught to despise more than any other in his world. The man was moving slightly, and groaning. With both legs broken he was just regaining consciousness and barely knew where he was. Slowly Lobo edged forward, drawn toward the odor he despised yet uncertain what to do. The snarl froze in his throat and hung there like a promise unfulfilled. It hung on like a living thing waiting to see if it was needed.

No more than three feet away from the badly injured

man Lobo sank down, first to his haunches, and then all the way down until his belly lay in the mud. He never once took his eyes off the man, he never once let his upper lip or his throat relax. Every muscle in his body was flexed, ready to move at the slightest sign of hostility.

An older wolf would have known what to do. Even Lobo, in the company of his parents, would have been likely to anticipate their command and would have moved off the moment the man's presence was detected. But Lobo alone—newly alone—was something else. Without his parents and without their training, here was something he had to resolve himself. Although hardly more than a cub, he had within him a well-schooled hatred of a particular sight, a special sound, a certain smell. Here, suddenly, were all of them, and their source, no more than a yard away.

Several times the man moved, groaned and tried to turn. With each movement Lobo was on his feet, backing away, a snarl on his lips. Once he nearly attacked when a particularly violent twitch was misinterpreted as the prelude to an attack. Somehow, although extreme caution was obviously called for, this thing that Lobo hated so much, this odor that walked upright was much less fearsome than a young wolf might have been led to expect. It seemed suddenly very vulnerable.

Finally Lobo got up enough nerve to inch forward. With teeth bared he slipped toward the helpless man and when close enough placed his paw on the man's shoulder. With this slightest pressure the man rolled toward the wolf, flopping grotesquely over on his back, his arms akimbo. Lobo stood over him now, his teeth only inches away from the man's bared throat. With his great yellow eyes Lobo looked down into the man's face, watched his quivering eyes open and saw the look of abject horror as the man's clouded mind managed to sort out his first impressions. Then, in what must rank as a most magnificent gesture of disdain, Lobo turned and, with his nostrils full of the stink of man, moved back down toward the southern end of the draw. Fifteen or twenty yards off he stopped, turned again and faced the man. Throwing his head straight back, pointing his muzzle to the sky, Lobo rolled his lament in a true wolf voice.

The man propped himself up on one elbow and stared in disbelief at the white apparition. Transfixed he watched the ghost-wolf sing, heard the strange timbre of his voice and formed an impression that would live not only in his own dreams but, spread afar, would live in fireside tales and even in recorded history. In that moment a legend was born.

Other men heard Lobo's call that day and spurred their horses forward. Lobo heard them as they entered the north end of the draw and turned his quest toward the south again. At the point of his original exit he turned toward the west, instead of the east, to which direction he had so miraculously escaped only a few hours before. Before moving more than a few dozen yards, however, he was again brought up short. There before him, as he moved hesitantly across the open ground, was the silver she-wolf. Half submerged in the mud, her head was twisted back, her bottom jaw missing, sliced off by a hoof and ground into the mud yards away. There was scarcely an inch of bone in her entire body that was intact; her skull had been crushed, her sides slit, her legs were barely attached. Her silver coat was smeared with her own blood and other internal substances.

Lobo had no trouble understanding what lay before him. Indeed, he had been weaned on death, for the wolf is not only a witness to the last phenomenon of life, he is an agent of it. He knew death well and was able to grasp the grosser facts. His mother lay dead. This was the body that had given him life and then sustained it with its nourishment. Although he could not understand his feelings he was as drawn to it as a human child is to his mother. Wolves may not love in the sense men love, but they love in their own way, and no one has yet shown that it is not as good.

If nature had given Lobo the power to cry, the ability to grieve, he would have flooded the prairie with his sorrow. But nature has given the wolf something else, and so once again Lobo went to his haunches, faced the heavens, and called to the world his woe of magnificent proportions. To all the poets among wolves who have ever lived, to all the gods who serve the kingdom of animals, to all that he was in fiber and in spirit, Lobo called. With exquisite skill he switched keys, picked up his own minor keys, and worked small miracles of musical intricacies.

Lobo's ode to the silver she-wolf echoed up through the draw and fell upon the ears of several men as they hunched over the man with the broken legs. There, as first aid was administered, the song of the wolf filled the night. Cursing, perhaps because he hated wolves, and perhaps only because he had found two men in the draw, one dead in the stampede and this other one sorely injured, one of the rescuers stood, walked to his horse, drew a rifle from its scabbard and walked toward the mouth of the draw. Standing back in the shadows, the man cast his expert, prairie-trained eyes far until they came to rest on the white wolf, sitting and calling. With a fading "Well, I'll be . . ." he brought his rifle to his shoulder, laid his cheek to the stock with the comfort and assurance of an experienced hunter, brought the base of Lobo's skull into confluence with the notch of the rear sight and the pole of the front, took up the slack in the trigger and squeezed off a round. The muzzle of the rifle leaped, the night parted, and a bullet, the first of many, was sent after Lobo. Once again the man cursed as he watched the white wolf—in what little was left of the late evening sun—move off at full speed. In years to come this story would change slightly; in these later versions, Lobo would continue his song, a ghost wolf impervious to bullets. But for the moment, the fact that this wolf was all white and sang with the voice of the devil was enough.

The next day, when the men came back to inspect the

damage the storm and the stampede had wrought, they found wolf tracks. They had the story of the man who had fired at a white wolf at point-blank range (and he, certainly, was an expert shot) ; they had the even more chilling first-hand account of the desperately injured man who swore he had fought the same wolf off with his bare hands; and since the man who had seen the actual start of the melee—had seen the tree hit by lightning—was dead, the story began that wolves, a white wolf in particular, had started the stampede.

In later versions, a wild pack of half-mad wolves would attack the heroic men on horseback and they would have to save themselves from being torn from their saddles and devoured. Indeed, they would slay many of the wolves before the attack subsided (the body of the silver wolf, after all, was found and this gave a certain credence to the tale).

Even as such stories were being born, a grand hunt was mounted to rid the county of wolves once and for all. Meanwhile, Lobo had moved away to another county, another part of the land, in search of food and a mate, and of his destiny as a wolf. He would never know the fate of his one remaining littermate. No one could tell him that the tan male too had survived the stampede, nor that he was soon trapped as the first and only true wolf victim in the grand wolf hunt that the legend of the ghost wolf had engendered.

With that, of the five wolves born in the deep excavation so many miles away, Lobo alone survived. His parents were dead, one reeking with the smell of man, the other full of the cattle stink. Lobo had seen both bodies, inspected them and filed away his impressions with great care. His filing system was perfect and his dual agony would be available from then on for immediate recall. The man whom Lobo inspected in the draw would be the only man who would ever see this wolf alive at close range. In the years to come, a river of blood would flow, and a complex of legends would grow up around this mysterious white wolf. The Custer Wolf had been born. Lobo the cub was a creature of the past.

ELEVEN

I T was 1914 and the white wolf was in his fifth year. Three maturing years had passed since he had walked away from his mother's decaying carcass on the flat South Dakota prairie, three years eventful not only in the life of this one animal but in the lives of many of the most impressive segments of North American wildlife.

If there is anything mankind likes better than a good, old-fashioned war, it is a mass of statistics that proves him right—or at least does not support an argument to the contrary. In the years of the Custer Wolf, mankind could satisfy both of these tastes. A predator himself, he went on a killing spree the likes of which had not been seen in this land since the days of the great bison hunts. He was fortified in his orgy of destruction, morcover, by as convenient and one-sided a collection of statistics as any that have ever been compiled. These self-serving figures showed that stockmen were losing between twenty and thirty million dollars per year to the accumulated stealth and hunting prowess of wolves, coyotes, pumas, bobcats and bears. Each wolf, it was reckoned by men with translucent green visors and black silk oversleeves, cost American ranchers and farmers a minimum of a thousand dollars a year. A wolf that lived ten years, by this figuring, was an expensive wildlife luxury.

By the time the Custer Wolf had reached his fifth year, traps, guns, and poison enough to wipe out every wolf that ever walked the face of the earth were stockpiled in the troubled areas. In the ensuing six years— 1915 through 1920—a sixteen-state war was waged that saw 128,513 assorted carcasses skinned and rotting in the sun. This represented but a fraction of the animals killed, of course, since the widespread and indiscriminate use of poisoned bait meant that uncounted additional thousands of animals had crawled away to die unnoticed. Of the thousands of large predators destroyed in these six fateful years, however, only 2936 were wolves. Texas, in characteristic bravado, led by offering up almost half of this total, with New Mexico, Wyoming and Montana following. In all of South Dakota's 77,047 square miles during those six years only 23 timber wolves are known to have been killed. (In the same period, South Dakota offered up the carcasses of 1 bear, 58 bobcats and lynxes and 794 coyotes, although not one mountain lion was taken. As a result of all this killing the rodent population exploded and in turn cost untold millions to bring under control.)

While these statistics, like all statistics, are good to have on hand for ready quoting, and although they may even be essential to our understanding of the world of the Custer Wolf, they mattered little to the great white animal himself. For while the statisticians in Washington assembled their facts, and the ranchers lamented their losses to the local predatory animal inspector of the federally maintained Biological Survey, the Custer Wolf had established a pattern of behavior that would earn him a place in the written history of the land. Ironically, his name was to outlive the names of the ranchers whose stock he raided.

He centered his hunting range on the town of Custer (seat of the southwestern county of Custer) and from there worked in a large circle forty to sixty-five miles or more in diameter. His great circular route became more erratic the longer he was pursued, but at various times it carried him through parts of Fall River, Custer, Pennington, Lawrence, Meade, Shannon, and (possibly) Butte counties. His tracks are said to have been found as well in Crook, Weston, and Niobrara counties in Wyoming. Whether or not he actually reached Nebraska during these last years is not really known.

The land through which he hunted was and is dramatic in its extremes. Blistering hot in the arid summer months, it becomes agonizingly cold in winter. Vast, flat expanses of tableland erupt suddenly into contorted shapes testifying to the power of erosion and the vulnerability of the very earth itself. He hunted through Jewel Cave National Monument and Wind Cave National Park. In the shadow of 7242-foot Harney Peak, the highest point in the state of South Dakota, he also hunted, and from there to the southeast into the vast Pine Ridge Indian Reservation and its tortured aridity.

The sound of his voice, strong but somehow filled with pathos, was heard in the Indian towns of Pine Ridge, Porcupine, and Wounded Knee (site of another kind of violence only twenty-five years earlier when the United States Army, to its everlasting disgrace, slaughtered men, women, and children of the Oglala Sioux who had gathered to engage in sacred rituals). There proud descendants of the once mighty Sioux, reduced to human rubble by the ambition of the settlers, nodded in approval at the sounds he made, for here at least was something remaining that was right and proper in the land. Here at least was one mighty hunter who had not bowed.

Across the White River he ranged, and on both banks of the Cheyenne. His distinctive prints were seen in the mud on the south bank of the Belle Fourche River and in all lands in between. He slipped silently through the splendid moonscapes of the Badlands, waiting until night before making the trek to avoid the awesome, furnace-like effect of the stark, sun-tortured walls. He hunted triumphantly in the Black Hills; and on the ranch lands of Richardson and Smith, Turner, Carter, Lawrence and Carroll, and dozens more, he worked his art and built about himself a legend that was soon to crystallize into an irresistible bounty figure. Before his story reached its end his name was known to people on the shores of both oceans and on the floor of Congress, and brought curses throughout his native land. So well known did he become, in fact, that his footprint was immediately recognizable to ranchers and hunters in the nine or ten counties where he is known or reputed to have hunted. More men could recognize on sight the print of his paw than have known the thumbprint of any of America's most infamous public enemies.

In the year 1916 the world of the Custer Wolf was plagued again with dreaded rabies, and coyotes once again were the major carriers. In that one year more than fifteen hundred people were attacked and bitten by rabid brush wolves, thus intensifying the hatred for wild canines that already gripped the land. From Mexico to Canada, from the Pacific Ocean to the shores of the Great Lakes, wolves, coyotes and foxes fell before the renewed and invigorated assault. In one incredibly dramatic gesture several running packs of wolfhounds were imported (from state-owned Russian stock recently liberated from tzarist bondage) and these regal creatures, with their arching backs and flowing pace, joined the hunt, albeit not too effectively.

No range rider set out in those days without a supply of strychnine in his kit. This product of the plant

Strychnos nux-vomica was available in every general store and druggist shop in the state. There was an unwritten law that allowed no rider to pass the carcass of a dead animal without baiting it. When no carcasses were to be found, animals were shot to provide them; and when there was nothing to shoot, the deadly tonic was imbedded in small balls and pellets of fat and strewn about to be found and consumed by an endless variety of harmless creatures. Everything from crows to badgers, mink to ferrets, foxes to skunks, otters, raccoons, and weasels were destroyed, not by the hundreds but by the thousands and, in some cases, tens of thousands.

It can only be guessed how many such fat pellets and baited carcasses the Custer Wolf scorned in his incredible survival of six years of this warfare. How he did it we can only approximate. His sense of smell, obviously, was remarkable and his nature very suspicious. These factors, combined with unimaginable other secret qualities, enabled him to survive while others all around him succumbed. It was as if a deadly hailstorm fell upon the land and this mythical white apparition alone knew how to survive it. A hundred times his tracks were found leading up to a baited steer or sheep, there to circle the remains several times before leading straight off at an arrogant pace. His tracks showed how he stepped over balls of poisoned fat without touching them—how, in fact, he thwarted every effort made to capture or kill him. It is not enough to say that he could smell the poison or could detect the odor of man, because other wolves, and thousands of coyotes, could not catch these vague clues. No, there was a special quality about this animal and no one who knew of him or his works would brook an argument on the subject—and he was often enough in those days a topic of conversation.

It was not the extent of the Custer Wolf's range, which was not extraordinary, nor his skill at eluding capture that earned him his unenviable reputation. In these regards he would not have drawn enough attention for it to have become known that it was one particular animal that was so often escaping. The reason was, in most sad fact, that he had deserted the ancient ways of the wolf and become a true renegade. The great white wolf killed, it seemed, for the pure joy of killing; indeed, his well-recorded depredations were astounding: in one night, thirty sheep, one partially eaten; in one night, ten head of steer, one partially eaten. Such were the reports that mounted on the desk of the Federal agent responsible for the area.

Even those who hate the wolf the most, if they know the animal at all, admit that such behavior is far from normal. Wolves are not normally killers-for-fun; the Custer Wolf apparently was. Wolves do not normally waste resources; the Custer Wolf did. He was in the purest sense a killer. Like the Indian and the bison he had been declared obsolete, but chose to stay on and fight a little longer in any way he could.

One does not have to look far in the hostile ring that encircled the world of the Custer Wolf to find reasons for his behavior. An animal so sensitively attuned to his environment could easily find reason to hate, reason enough to launch a private war on those he could certainly recognize as his enemies. It is doubtful, though, that a wolf, even this one, could be capable of so complex an emotion as revenge. That, surely, followed toolmaking as an invention of man. But perhaps there is a more primitive kind of revenge, a pattern of behavior similar to that engendered by revenge in man, but of simpler structure. Perhaps the Custer Wolf *hated*. Perhaps his response patterns were conditioned to react violently to the stimulation of certain odors and, being a predator, he killed in response to them.

Perhaps it is reaching too far to say that the Custer Wolf hated. Perhaps it was even less complex than that. But whatever the reason, such was the behavior of the Custer Wolf, and sad was the record of waste he spread across his land. Few wolves in history have been worse, or even as bad.

T W E L V E

To those who derive their entire life from the land directly and immediately, no two places on this planet are at all alike. To higher forms who speed by in cars and buses, there may be a sameness to a prairie, and one rolling hill might look like the rest. That is only because of the space and time they have created to shield themselves from their past and from the present realities of the natural order of life. Every can of bleached and preserved fruit a man opens, every cellophane-wrapped package of processed food that is 50 per cent farm and 50 per cent laboratory-factory removes him yet another step from the only world the wolf can ever know.

For the wolf, and especially for so highly skilled a hunter as the Custer Wolf, the range in its infinite scapes is an intimate thing. Its shape and form, its mantle of life, all gave forth messages that enabled the white wolf to orient himself. He knew it well, by sight, by sound, by smell, and certainly by feel. He not only knew where he was but immediately knew the season and therefore the hunting potentials of any given area. No hill was at all like any other, no tree the same as even another of the same species sprung from seeds germinated in the same year, and no gully, valley, cut, or draw remotely like any of the millions of others on this entire planet. To know this, to understand and to be able to navigate by it, one needs only the ears, eyes, nose, and intelligence of a wolf.

On this night the white wolf moved onto lands he had not seen for over two months. In that period he had wandered over six hundred miles through parts of six counties; every foot he traversed was twelve inches of danger. Hunted, pursued, ambushed, his every moment was guarded, pre-calculated. He took few direct actions without first overlaying the required measure of deceit. Always there was the zigzag course, the indirect approach; distances of five miles could seldom be covered in fewer than seven or eight because of the need to lay false trails. Rivers were swum dozens of times more than was made necessary by geography, because of his hunters and the demands they made upon him.

Even a recent spring rain that had lasted more than twelve hours had not altered the tone of the land so much that the Custer Wolf did not know immediately where he was. Gliding through a small wood and into the open near a split rail fence, he knew immediately where the pasture lay, where the dangerous bulls would be penned and where the vulnerable heifers moved in relative freedom. Skirting the direct light of the moon by moving within the projected image of a high cloud, he traveled across the open, flat pasture and sought momentary shelter beside a water trough. His white coat, while lending much to the legends that were built up around him, was genetically a mistake. He was too obvious in the moonlight and found it difficult to seek quick, emergency cover. In the far North, on Arctic tundra where snow is the normal scene for most of the year, his color would have been a decided advantage. Here, though, on green, gray, brown and black prairie, where men had guns that shot far and well, it was a natural error that would soon eliminate itself by the pattern of survival and reproduction. Individually he was an obsolete animal and a member of an obsolete species. Here, where men had their hate, it was so ordered.

Crouching in the shadow of the wooden trough, the white wolf performed the magic of the night hunter. He detached his senses from the prison of self and set them moving across the land. The pupils of his great, yellow eyes dilated and each stray wisp of light reflected from great mirror cells at the back of his eyes, deep in his skull, and bounced its register onto his sensitive brain. Little that existed and nothing that moved would escape his notice, even where clouds shadowed the land from the full moon. His ears were erect, sensitively turning on their axis, shifting forward and back, seeking in fine adjustment the first hint of alien sound. There were horses at the far end of the pasture but their nervous footfall was natural. Had a horse with rider come into the area, the wolf would have been immediately alerted. A horse steps differently when burdened, and saddle leather creaks in a way the Custer Wolf would not have missed.

While his sight and hearing sought out the pockets and secrets of the night his sense of smell asked questions of every current of air, intruded itself not only into the activities of the hour but recalled the many hours of the preceding days. He could tell who and what had passed; he could reconstruct their actions and, in many cases, even their moods. Once again we must acknowledge the possibility of yet another way in which the white wolf dissected the night. Besides the probings of his eyes, ears, and snout there may have been another tool. Perhaps the nearest we can come to it is to say that the Custer Wolf *felt* the night. Whether it was a sixth (or seventh) sense, some supernatural quality, or one so natural that we must be fools not to understand it, we cannot truly know.

This supposed quality of the wolf's senses has fascinated man for ages and led to wondrous fictions. The peasants of much of rural Sweden are so sure of this power that they attribute magical qualities to it and will not even speak the word *wolf* for fear of what might befall them. He is called *gray one* or *old gray*, but never by his proper name. To the ancient Romans he was a fruitful source of augury and his actions were carefully watched, faithfully interpreted. A Roman military emplacement visited by a wolf that had escaped unhurt was plunged into despair, for surely that meant impending defeat and enslavement. It is even said that the tragic results of the Punic War were brought about (or at least foretold) by a wolf that had entered an army camp and carried off a sentry's sword. These stories, and thousands more like them, have lived down through the centuries as by-products of the wolf's skill as a hunter; a more oafish fellow would have earned less of a reputation—if, indeed, he was able to survive at all. Such stories and legends, however, added to the dread which the presence of the Custer Wolf engendered and helped to justify the attitudes and actions of men where he was concerned. Unhappily, neither the wolf nor any of his kind could ever have the intelligence to deal with abstracts like legends and stories. Theirs was, and is, a more elemental world than that.

By now, at the far end of the pasture, the fact of the wolf's presence had slowly dawned on a small cluster of mares. A foggy mist had been swept away from their insufficient brains, allowing this information to register; and thus, as their low powers of absorption struggled against their ignorance, their nervousness mounted. Their feet now made frantic movements in the manure-laden soil, and the drumming of their hooves told the Custer Wolf immediately what he wanted to know—that he had been detected, that a treacherous little wind had shifted and thrown his secret back at the horses just as it had carried theirs to him.

Well aware that such frightened animals usually brought men, dogs and guns quickly on the scene, the Custer Wolf slid underneath a fence, found an avenue of shadow and moved away from the hysteria of the horses. Before their neighs and snorting would be heard at the ranch house, and before lights would come on giving farmhouse and bunkhouse great yellow eyes of their own with which to look out upon the night, he would be a full mile away. By the time men, dogs and guns had reached the horses and had determined that they were unharmed, he would have made his kill elsewhere. By the time the hounds would find his trail, he would have eaten enough for that night and the next day. He was in the practice of eating quickly, and quite used to wasting 90 per cent or more of what he destroyed.

As the white wolf slid under the lower rail of the fence in the back pasture, a full mile from the nervously prancing mares, a dark shape loomed up before him. The steam and dust that rose from it like a cloud marked it unmistakably as a cow; at five times the distance the Custer Wolf would have been able to make the same observation. The cow's head hung low as she slumbered in reeking contentment amid her comfortable world of plenty. Descended from wild oxen tough enough to put a whole pack of wolves to flight, cousin to the fighting bulls of Spain and Mexico, this great, heaving milk machine lived in somnambulent splendor, hardly conscious of the world around her. She was the genetic creation of man, so altered from an original form as to be hardly recognizable as having arisen from something wild and graceful. She was man-made as surely as a loaf of bread or a custard pudding, and her purpose and her personality were about the same.

Quickly scanning the field of battle, rapidly absorbing and processing all impulses, the white wolf moved toward the form. Just as the cow's numb brain began to sense the danger, just as she started to turn to stare at the approaching wolf with slack-jawed disbelief, he went into action. Breaking into a full run, swinging sideways at the last moment, he cut across the front of the stationary cow, swung his head upright and, with hardly a wasted effort, imbedded his canines into her throat; his nose thrust forward and down, and he felt her blood start to empty upon the ground as it flowed across his muzzle, blinding him momentarily. He turned away, out from under the cow's heavy chin, and watched her front legs fold as she went to her knees. Her rear legs remained extended, giving her back a precarious slope, and she began to cough with a strange hollow sound. Even in the dark it could be seen that the ground beneath her was being stained a deep, dark shade.

Finally, with ease and assurance, the Custer Wolf walked over to her, put his forefeet on her shoulders and leaned forward. The cow tumbled, lay on her side, and slowly died. By the time her last breath had faded in a guttural splutter the white wolf was opening her paunch to get at her unborn calf. It was his love for this delicacy, as much as any other single trait he had developed down through the years, that caused him to be one of the most hated individual animals this land has ever known.

THIRTEEN

M ANY years ago, science found a way of identifying
and cataloging the plants and animals of both
the past and the present. Once apparent family rela-
tionships are established and likely evolutionary se-
quence determined, animals are given scientific names
approved by an international body of specialists. Although it is always under attack and constantly having
even some of its basic philosophies challenged, it is the
nearest thing to a workable system man seems able to
achieve. It is, in short, imperfect but good. Buried
within the hundreds of thousands of such Latin and
Greek-derived words a place for the Custer Wolf can be
found. The timber wolf is a member of the species *Canis*

lupus. His first name, *Canis,* denotes his genus and from it we can readily determine who his closest relatives are. Science lists the other members of *Canis* as the red wolf, now only of the American south-central region, the domestic dog, the Australian dingo, the jackals of Africa and Asia, and the brush wolf, or coyote. Within the immediate world of the Custer Wolf he had to contend only with domestic dogs, no doubt sired by his own ancestors, and coyotes.

There was good reason for the white wolf to hate the sight, smell, or sound of the domestic dog, all of which were taught to dread the wolf and play the tocsin at his appearance. Indeed, the domestic dog probably gave him more discomfort in the course of his life than any other single weapon in the not inconsiderable arsenal of man. His shallow voice and poor music (when compared with that of the wolf) always heralded trouble. On many a moonlit night and dark, the white wolf had fled like a thief before the baying, barking and whining of the hounds.

Whether or not the enmity between wolf and dog was all man-inspired is somewhat difficult to determine. Although wolves can and occasionally do breed with domestic dogs, they also attack and kill them just as a pack of dogs will trail and attack a wolf if given the chance. That two so closely related animals, not competing for food or a mate under anything approaching normal circumstances, should so violently hate each other is rather strange. One would think that dogs, as sociable as wolves by nature, might summon up within them a wondrous nostalgia at the first wolf sign; but such is not the case—it certainly was not the case during the time of the Custer Wolf.

The wolf's relationship to the coyote is something else. The coyote does not carry with it the sign of man and is, in fact, as much persecuted as the wolf. Evidence has been found in Canada that suggests that wolves and coyotes can successfully mate, although it is most doubtful that this happens in the wild state in any but the rarest instances, if at all. In times of scarcity, when the resources of the earth seem to shrivel and die, a wolf will attack and kill a coyote for food, just as he will almost any other animal. Likewise, scavenging coyotes will, no doubt, attack and finish off a sick or injured wolf unable to defend himself. But these circumstances seem to be more the exception than the rule; the average wolf lives in fair tolerance with the average coyote. They do not often associate closely, but neither do they go out of their way to harm or interfere with each other.

All this was generally known to those who had reason to think about the wolf in the years 1915 to 1920. It was the more startling, then, to learn that the familiar tracks of the Custer Wolf were being found in close proximity to those of two coyotes. At first, there was no way to be sure that an actual association existed, for it could have been coincidence—the wolf and the coyotes might simply have been passing the same way hours or even minutes apart. Unless a weather condition, such as a rain or dust storm, should intervene between the two

events even the most expert tracker would find it extremely difficult to date a track down to the hour. Still,
the story spread that the Custer Wolf, by now 90 per
cent legend and only 10 per cent animal, had taken up
with two coyotes. The outlaw had gotten himself a
gang, so to speak, and the havoc they would now wreak,
it was predicted, would exceed anything the prairie
country had ever known.

Throughout his entire life the Custer Wolf was so
rarely seen by human beings that it was no reflection on
the story that he was not regularly seen with his coyote
companions. He was, after all, known from his tracks
and by his deeds, seldom by firsthand observation. On
one occasion, however, the story of the white wolf and
his coyotes was bolstered by human observation. An un-
named ranch hand rode up over a slight rise just at
dusk one day and saw a white wolf coursing away across
a small valley with two coyotes running out in front and
slightly to the sides. Like outriders they ran and seemed
to know where the white animal wanted to go. The
slanting rays of the retiring sun cast a ghostly light
over all and the rider reported the strange scene to some
friends a few days hence. The rider's name and further
details of the event are lost to us now.

Wolves were scarce enough in South Dakota at that
time for it to be assumed that a wolf howl at night could
be linked with tracks found the next morning. It was
unlikely that two wolves would be in the same area at
the same time unless both their voices were heard. On a
number of occasions, when tracks known to belong to

the white wolf were found close by those of two coyotes, the call of a wolf could be heard at night answered only by the distinctive, yapping coyote howl. No other wolf was there to answer, and the lonely sounds, at once sad and exhilarating for the human listener, were heard sounding against the night, trying the dark hours for secrets in reply.

During his presumed association with the two coyotes, and even after they were taken away from him, the white wolf practiced a second insult against the fortunes and sacrosanct properties of man that caused extreme anger among his foes. He bobtailed cattle.

The practice of bobtailing cattle, or amputating their tails, is not an uncommon practice with wolves. The phenomenon, listed under the generic heading of mutilation, has been reported often enough. It has been the belief of many that the practice is most common with female wolves teaching their cubs how to stop a cow or steer from getting away. Other reports have wolves hanging from steers' tails exuberantly enjoying a free ride, like naughty boys hitching onto the tailgate of a passing truck. (Since photographs reveal tails neatly bitten off where they had joined the body, these explanations don't seem to satisfy the facts as they apparently exist.)

For whatever reason and by whatever physical means, the Custer Wolf did engage in extensive mutilation during certain periods of his life. Not only were tails amputated but sides were slit, hunks were bitten off flanks and shoulders, and other forms of lesser damage done. These were not the marks left on victims he failed to kill—he could have killed any one of the animals so mutilated if he chose—but represented pure, mischievous damage without reason or purpose and were doubly infuriating to the owners of the stock that had been so badly treated.

On some raids the great white animal would strike like lightning, singling out one animal and quickly killing it for food. On other nights, for no apparent reason, he would gnash his way across a pasture, or even a farmyard, killing everything there. On still other occasions he would range back and forth through a livestock enclosure, mutilating but not killing everything in sight. And there were times when he would pass through a valley and, in one night, kill quickly and disappear long before any effort could be made to apprehend him; or he might simply take up peaceful resi dence in an area and taunt the local hunters and their dogs until the air turned blue at the mention of his name.

It does seem in retrospect—although we can say for certain this was not the case—that several distinct intellectual processes were involved, as if the renegade Custer Wolf had made his mind up to something. It was as if he knew his days were numbered, and that he would never see his normal span of fourteen to sixteen years before being caught; that therefore he had decided to even a very lopsided score with the men and cattle who had taken over his range and declared him outlaw in his own ancestral hunting grounds. We could almost believe that this renegade wolf knew that by acting erratically, by constantly changing his pattern of behavior, he could best confound his foes and elude their increasing fervor. He seemed to sense the mounting clamor.

However much we want to explain his actions in those days of his increasing madness, we cannot do it in terms of purely human emotional or intellectual patterns. Certainly there was some kind of primitive instinct that taught him how to confound and confuse those who would have his hide by changing his tactics day by day and hour by hour. How little or how much the coyotes figured in his life is not known. But it is an exciting image—these smaller brush wolves running ahead as outriders—and perhaps their part in his life has been exaggerated because it is so pleasing, so dramatically "right." In fact though, they were probably little more than parasites that he learned to tolerate in the extreme of his loneliness. Perhaps they served some purpose in that regard, but in little other. Eventually their lives both ended in traps that had been set for their white companion—and one can but wonder if the white wolf even sensed their passing.

FOURTEEN

S OMEHOW, in virtually all matters, man eventually manages to express his evaluation of the situation in terms of dollars and cents. You can often measure a man's love for—or guilt over—a deceased relative by the size of the headstone he erects. Indeed, that is how it is calculated: to look expensive. The cost of the gift a man gives to his wife, for another example, is often indicative of the size of his guilt. Somehow a price tag gets attached to just about everything we touch. And so it inevitably happened that a dollar value was placed on the exasperation the white wolf had engendered. His crimes, frustrating and demoralizing to those who claimed to rule the land, were eventually tagged with a dollar size and his life was given a special dollar value.

It has been estimated that during his last six years the Custer Wolf destroyed in excess of $25,000 worth of livestock in South Dakota. Toward the end of his career many ranchers gave up in despair and began figuring out the possible age of the killer. They resigned themselves to feeding him as long as he lived and began to pray for an early natural death—since he was obviously immune to any unnatural ones they might devise.

At that time the bounty on an adult wolf ran as high as $50 ($20 for a cub) ; it varied from place to place, of course, but those are round medium figures. By the time the Custer Wolf reached the peak of his eventful career, the price on his head was ten times normal—$500. Having thus established the safe and reliable standard of the dollar for their anger, the ranchers waited for the takers to arrive—and with good reason. In South Dakota in the years of World War I, $500 was a great deal of money.

And so from far and wide they came, sliding out of hidden pockets in the wolf's own hunting range. They came in beat-up old cars, on horseback, in wagons, some carrying homemade rifles that looked more deadly to the hunter than his target, others armed with surgically precise English double rifles worth thousands. They arrived with lures, scents, brews and broths of incredible aroma, and proceeded to create clouds of noxious gas that fairly hovered overhead. (There was a standing joke at the time to the effect that if you stood still on this open prairie for more than ten minutes some expert would come along and declare you one of the white wolf's scent posts.) Traps of every possible description were unlimbered: dead falls, nooses, logs with spears imbedded hung high ready to fall, and pits with spears imbedded waiting to receive the falling; bear traps and wolf traps, ancient and new, traps conceived in universities and concocted in garages, they were all at hand.

Men with red beards and blue eyes—and men with red eyes and blue vocabulary—poured across the land. They were welcomed at any ranch, for hospitality was boundless and free. There was always room in the bunkhouse, always food enough at each groaning board. If you said that you came to get the white wolf, you were treated, like the rainmaker, with respect and awe.

And yet, when the ancient Indian incantations (usually concocted on the spot) were finished, when the Rube Goldberg contraptions were packed off or abandoned to rust in the eventual prairie rains, the Custer Wolf was still at large, wandering his range supremely free and twice as arrogant. He raided ever closer to ranch house and village outskirts, and returned to punish the same places again and again. Through it all, no trap was sprung by his foot, no baited carcass or fatball touched. No clear rifle shot was ever had. (Although a number were claimed, it is absolutely astounding how many times cooperative winds blew stinging particles of sand into the eyes of hunters just as they

lined up on a sure shot.) Those who shot from horseback were often unaccountably thrown off their aim by
a horse that suddenly bolted. Indeed, the white wolf was
charmed—if indeed he was a living animal at all.

Delegations went down into the Indian towns, with
their pride tucked away where it wouldn't show, and
asked advice of the old men of the tribe. Surely the
mighty Sioux would know how to deal with such a devil!
The old Indians shook their heads and looked at the
dust on the ground. *No, not that one. Nothing can get
that one.*

The ranchers should have known for whom the Sioux
would cheer. Whatever price they paid themselves in
the loss of a few miserable sheep and goats the Indians
would gladly accept. The Custer Wolf was too much a
part of the Sioux for them to contribute to his downfall.
Indians then still alive remembered well the night when
the women wept and the children cried for dead parents.
No, the Sioux would not give the answer, and on the
porch of the general store in Wounded Knee—a hundred yards from where a monument now stands admit-
ting to the senseless slaughter—old men sat and mum-
bled, chuckling every now and then. Even the white
wolf had a cheering section.

And so the word spread, down into old Mexico, into
the border towns and the cantinas, up into Canada
where prospectors still scratched at the earth like chickens looking for gold, west to the Pacific and back East
to the posh hunting and gun clubs. Here in the United
States, at a time when cars were common and air travel

was predicted for everyone, there existed an old-time Western villain. He had his gang, and he had his tricks, and he drenched the ground with blood on every witch's Sabbath. The word spread and the hunters came; for six years it went on and still the Custer Wolf was without his first scar. Many began to doubt that he existed and began to look for the smart turn of a promoter's hand.

The Custer Wolf did exist, however, and he was both white in color and renegade killer at heart. Whatever endearing traits he may have had as a cub, however much like a gangling dog he may once have looked, by the time he reached his tenth and last year the Custer Wolf was an animal who deserved destruction. He had forgotten how to live with anybody or anything, a killer wolf for whom neither nature nor man had any use. There was no niche for him to fill.

FIFTEEN

I N March of 1920 the renegade career of the Custer Wolf reached its peak and there began the last act of a rare and still unexplained wildlife drama. The ranchers of the counties wherein he raided had all but given up. *A wolf doesn't live forever*, they said, as they resigned themselves to a few more years of shattering financial losses.

Hunters, trappers and medicine men had been coming and going for years and, in these last months of the white wolf's reign of terror, they attracted less attention than they had earlier. Thus, when professional hunter H. P. Williams arrived on the scene in March, he was accepted as just one more man having a well-intentioned go at the $500 bounty. Williams, tall and youthful-looking, was exceptionally skilled and set about his work with a minimum of fuss. He was accorded little special attention by the ranchers and none at all by the Custer Wolf.

Earlier in the same year Williams had earned a certain amount of fame in Wyoming by ridding that state of the Split Rock Wolf, a killer that had cost ranchers an estimated $10,000 in livestock. Like the white wolf, he had proven far too elusive for the average trapper and had been deemed invincible by the many who had tried to get him. But Williams had tracked him down and earned the reputation of being a master hunter. A few men called his success luck and suggested he would come to naught if ever he took on the Custer Wolf. Whether or not Williams heard those remarks and took the Custer Wolf on to disprove them we cannot say. For one reason or another, he showed up in southwestern South Dakota in March and went to work. His stay was to last through October.

Reports of the white wolf were not long in coming. On a cool Sunday night he slipped over the boundary line of a large holding in Fall River County, not far from the town of Hot Springs, and killed a prize ram. He passed up several other rams nearby, made his one kill, and fed until some dogs got his scent and set up a wailing and a moaning that brought the lights blinking on in every room in the ranch house. Before anything could be done, he had dissolved into the night. (A report from the town of Martin in Bennett County, close to a hundred miles away, indicating that the white wolf had struck there on the same night was obviously in error.)

Two nights after he struck near Hot Springs, he took a heifer near Edgemont. Again a single clean kill was made and part was eaten. In the few weeks that followed his kills were single, for the purposes of food, and not attention-getting by themselves. It was the Custer Wolf's distinctive footmark near the kills that attracted the special notice.

Following these several weeks of relative calm, the white wolf suddenly dropped from view. Calls and telegrams failed to turn up a single report of a kill made by him and rumors started that had him dead, captive, mated, or off in other states—Nebraska, Wyoming, Montana, North Dakota, even Texas. In fact, it is probably safe to assume that he merely moved off into some back country and lived off the spring crop of young wild animals. There were then, as now, pronghorn, bison and deer in the state, and the outlaw was perhaps enjoying a simple change in diet. No scribes recorded his kills during this period, for nature keeps no such records.

But just when the rumors of his death were picking up speed in their race across South Dakota, the white wolf reappeared. He struck near Rapid City in Pennington County and killed thirty head of stock within a week. Then, while the hunters focused their attention on that area, he moved south and, outside the town of Custer, killed two horses. The sound of their terrified whinnying brought guns, dogs and hunters in the middle of the night, and as the moon peeked out from behind a cloud for a fleeting instant, one of the hunters swore he saw a wolf twice the size of any other and white as snow slip away between some trees.

The fact that the Custer Wolf's paw print was of average size did not in any way interfere with the story that now grew up about his being a giant as well as a lustful killer. This legend was further enhanced a few nights later, after he had killed the two horses, when the report came down through two-, three-, and four-party lines that the Custer Wolf had at last threatened human life down near the southeast corner of the state. Near the spot where Fall River, Shannon, and Custer counties meet, an unarmed ranch hand rode out to look for some strays when he is said to have come upon a white wolf the size of a pony. The great brute of an animal, it was reported, rose up, raised his mane, curled his lips back (revealing teeth that could rival those of a saber-toothed tiger), and brought forth a snarl that shook the very ground and all but paralyzed the rider and his horse. Sparks shot out of the dread figure's eyes and saliva ran from his mouth in quantities profound enough to make little pools at his feet—but, by the greatest good luck, and by riding his horse to death, the rider managed to escape.

This alleged incident is said to have taken place just before nightfall, so presumably the ranch hand had a good look at the white wolf, thus becoming one of the few men ever to do so. The fact that the Custer Wolf did, in fact, make a single kill that same day west of Custer, some fifty-odd miles from the scene of the eye-witnessing, did not destroy the legend; whether the rider saw a coyote that evening, or actually encountered another wolf, is a secret that must be held by him. In actual fact, however, the Custer Wolf is not known to have ever threatened a human being.

Meanwhile, as Williams and the other hunters moved back and forth through the Custer Wolf's hunting range, they were acting out an ancient drama. Although the wolf is an animal seldom given to wild killing orgies, renegades have cropped up from time to time in the history of this land. In each case they were the notable exception; indeed, the exceptional quality of their acts served to underscore how unspectacular the average wolf is. In the centuries of settlement this land has known, and among the tens and hundreds of thousands of wolves that have come, acted out their allotted life, and gone, only a few have come down to us in the written records as renegades, senseless killers more involved in staining the soil red with blood than in feeding their cubs and their mates.

In 1739, General Israel Putnam, a hero of the Revolution, became engaged in a bitter war with a she-wolf that raided his farm forty miles east of Hartford, Connecticut. In one night the killer took seventy-five of his sheep and goats, and wounded many more. Eventually Old Put's Wolf, as he was known, paid the price and became one of the earliest dead renegades in American history.

In southern Oregon the famed Sycan Wolf held ranchers at his mercy for twelve years before he was finally trapped near Fort Klamath. Between 1889 and 1894, the so-called Currumpaw region of New Mexico suffered disastrous livestock losses to a hundred-and-fifty-pound male wolf before he, too, fell to a skilled hunter. And in Montana, the infamous Pryor Creek Wolf took a special liking to Shetland ponies, adding them to his steady diet of horse, mule, milk cow and steer whenever he had the chance. Another renegade, known as the Aguila Wolf, ranged the desert country of Arizona not far from Wickenburg during the peak years of the Custer Wolf's rampage. Like the Custer Wolf, he would go suddenly berserk and on at least one occasion killed sixty-five sheep between the hours of sunset and sunrise. On another night soon after that, he killed forty.

In South Dakota, during the same years, another renegade killer—known to history as Three Toes of Harding County—outlasted the white wolf by five years. During his thirteen-year rampage, fully 150 hunters were on his trail; in one two-night foray he killed 66 head of cattle. In Colorado, the eight-year killing spree of Old Lefty ended in a trap in 1913. He is known to have killed at least 384 head of livestock. Old Whitey, another Colorado renegade, was one of the worst bobtailers this country has ever known. He was a free-ranging killer for fifteen years before being taken. Still another famous killer from Colorado was Rags the

Digger, who, like the others, eventually paid with his life.

H. P. Williams and the other hunters who were after the Custer Wolf knew of these animals and of many more as well. The stories about Unaweep Wolf and Big Foot, the Phantom of Fruita and the Greenhorn Wolf, of Three Toes of the Apishapa, the Traveler, Old Guy Jumbo, Old Doctor, the Black Devil, Peg Leg, all these and a dozen more were necessary information for the men who made their living by ridding the land of such scourges. Each animal had his individual traits, but all had certain characteristics in common. It was the knowledge of these common characteristics that proved invaluable to the hunter. The Custer Wolf, exceptional though he may have been as an individual, was no different in this regard and Williams was convinced he would eventually take him, just as he had the Split Rock Wolf and many lesser outlaws.

Of the many stories about the white wolf that have come down to us, often told by men who were then alive and who heard the stories fresh and new, many are of course quite false, or at least terribly exaggerated. But one strange story that is often told was apparently true, for photographic records exist, along with expert testimony. It began when Williams, thinking that horse scent might be too revealing, apparently spent part of his time tracking the white wolf on foot. Working on a trail not far south of Custer, shortly after the wolf had made a particularly devastating raid, Williams painted the bottoms of his boots with a fresh

batch of wolf scent, which had been made from the remains of a she-wolf captured a short time before.

During his half decade or more near Custer, the
white wolf is not known to have had a mate. His lonely,
unanswered wailings, his association—however brief and
fleeting—with two coyotes, and the lack of other tracks
all point to a sad, bachelor life. So unnatural a life is
bound to have had some effect on the animal, because he
was not made by nature to live alone. All his instincts,
all his inner urgings and promptings pointed him in a
quite different direction. How much his renegade life
resulted from his being unmated, or how much his celi-
bate life was the responsibility of his outlaw ways cannot be calculated. Perhaps both were the products of
chance.

In any event, it is known the Custer Wolf sorely
longed for a mate. And on at least this one occasion he
gave pathetic proof of how unfit he was to live the life
that was forced upon him. For somewhere on his travels
near the center of his range he crossed Williams's trail
and picked up the new wolf scent the hunter was using
on his boots. It is certain that he imagined an exciting
new she-wolf had entered his territory, for during the
ensuing days he acted in a way he had never done
before and was never to do again. He began tracking
Williams! Instead of fleeing, as was his normal course,
he often came very close to the hunter, though never
close enough to be seen.

Somehow, in some strange way, deep-rooted instincts
were released; for the first time sexual behavior natural

to the normal wolf, but held prisoner within this white animal by the very powers that made him an outlaw, flowed freely. Picking a dry gully about twenty miles southwest of the town of Custer, the Custer Wolf began to prepare, incredible as it seems, for the coming of his cubs. Strange and sad it was that his phantom mate was long since dead, that she lingered on only as a scent on the bottoms of H. P. Williams's boots.

The draw he selected ran deep into the dry dirt of South Dakota. The white wolf chose a spot high up near the rim of the draw and began to dig. Night and day he drove himself deeper into the earth until his paws were raw. Several times he had to leave his den site and seek food and water, but he was soon back and digging. When hunters eventually found his unused den and measured it they found a vacant hole running fifty feet into the earth. After completing so mammoth an undertaking, after digging so furiously and removing so many hundreds of pounds of earth, how long did he wait for his mate? How many nights and how many days did the white wolf give of those last weeks of his life in search of a family that existed only within the foundries of his own instincts and in the faint smell of a long dead she-wolf? Surely his howling on those nights, the song he sang to his lonely urgings, was among the saddest of sounds and the most ironic of laments.

That fifty-foot excavation, now long since collapsed and lost to view, must stand in a few musty old photographs and in a few written accounts as a testimony to the loneliness of the life of crime. The Custer Wolf, like so many of his human counterparts, paid one of the gravest prices of all. At best his was a life of lonely despair and unfulfilled demands made upon him by an insistent heritage without regard for the hopelessness of his position.

SIXTEEN

T HE land and all that it contained yearned for another season. The sun, author of life and sustainer
of all that lived, moved erratically into a period of
merciless extremes and smashed its searing heat against
the earth. Moisture was drawn out of all that was
exposed and sent off on other errands. With imbalance
and irony, water so desperately needed in one place was
called away by the white heat and hastened off to
rendezvous on mountaintops with snow already thousands of feet deep, or to lie upon the surface of an ocean
without need of the offering.

In towns reasonably well protected by reservoirs and
deep wells, photographers took pictures of eggs frying

on sidewalks and hastened their visual clichés off to the presses of larger cities. Farmers, with greater needs and more to lose, fretted and grew more irritable with each rainless day. Animals, with their very lives at stake, panted or sweated, each in his own way, with eyes averted from the blinding sun.

In the gullies and cuts where water lately ran the dryness took on a pattern and the earth, turning to mud in the last hours of its moisture, cracked and split with each little odd-shaped wedge, turning up at the edges to become earthen knives waiting for sensitive pads and suffering paws. There was a white, sand-blasted stillness aloft and black, feathered forms lazily circled, slipping in and out of the glare as if behind curtains and clouds. Death was a presence with a personality, not just an eventuality.

The Custer Wolf, awesome in so many other ways, was as much a victim of the summer extreme as any other creature. He lay up under a ledge in a jumble of time-resistant rock in the middle of a plain and panted the hours of the heat away. His tissues were no less water-constituted than others of his kind and his body suffered no less. The heat from above flattened him against the earth. His coat fell away in chunks and wisps of down from his undercoat caught on every rock he brushed against and lay waiting for the slightest hint of wind. Each passing breeze carried something of his winter pelt away until he was tattered and ragged like a discarded toy. He was still a wolf, but now a used one.

His high shelter offered more than shade; from it he

commanded a view. His yellow eyes, raw and stinging from the bitter heat and the sand, could rest upon miles of flat land without his stirring. By whatever means a wolf has of knowing that a situation vaster than the moment exists, the white wolf now knew that he was being hunted. A hunter himself, he knew what a recurring scent meant each time he circled and crossed his own trail and found it lying over his own. To say that he consciously understood what was going on is perhaps to go too far. But even without that understanding he knew how to respond; a five-mile trek that would have been eight miles long before now stretched to ten. When waterways were encountered—those that had not given all to the sun—he entered their shallows and traveled for miles before emerging onto dry land. He chose hard rock rubble, although it was crueler to his feet than softer matrices, and strove to leave as little behind him as possible. In time, his skill had increased so that he could roll his traces up and carry them off with him as he did his own shadow. Everything, that is, but his odor.

There was, however, one other track he lay down that was as easily followed by a man as his scent was by a hound: his hunting pattern. The more hostile he became —if we can assume that hostility played a part in his deeds—the more readily his name could be read in the trail of blood and offal he left behind. His restricted range and the process of elimination combined to mark his kills as his own and he was referred to simply as "he." Everyone knew to whom the reference was made.

On this particular blistering day, from his high vantage point the white wolf watched a dark form pick its way slowly across the open land. A rumbling sound he had come to associate with the stink of rubber and gas drifted up to him and faded and grew with the caprices of rising thermals. The first time he saw such a form move along a road he had crouched in a ditch nearby and fairly quaked in terror. He had to fight to control his instincts to run. Rather than expose himself he had waited it out; but for days after he was shy and he did not hunt on ranch land for nearly a week. On another occasion, when he watched hounds unload from such a shape, he had retreated into a secret ravine and again laid up for several days. From each of these experiences, and several more that followed, he learned one important fact: cars and trucks were to be feared and avoided, even if not understood. They belonged with man—just as dogs, cattle, traps, poison and guns did.

Far more deadly than a car with a hunter passing by is a car with a hunter that fails to pass by. When the lumbering, wheezing, snorting shape stopped at the foot of the hill the white wolf was on his feet. All heat was forgotten, for here was a more immediate concern. As the door of the truck opened, the wolf lay back slightly, his lip twitching in prelude to a snarl. He watched with unblinking interest as the man cast about and found a single, broad track in a mound of soft dust that he had traversed earlier to reach the rock jumble. He watched as the man looked up, squinted his eyes against the sun, then shielded them with his arm and looked directly at him. Their eyes met for an instant, although the man was never to know it; with the sun behind him, crouched in the midst of bleached rock and meaningless shadows, the white wolf was as invisible as if he had been endowed with the powers men gave to him in their stories.

Hoping that the wolf had chosen a den that ran deep into the hill, and thus had not noticed his approach, the man began scanning the rocks for likely sites before starting to climb. The wolf watched until the man had slipped from sight behind a large outcropping, then turned to descend the hill by a secret way.

Eventually the man reached the spot where the wolf had rested and knelt to seek confirming signs. He found the hollow that had been dug in search of moisture and cool earth, and he found the bits of wool from the shedding undercoat. As he crept forward on his knees to test the vantage point and admire the choice the wolf had made he saw what he thought was a form slip out from between two rocks at the very foot of the hill. For a moment he was certain, and then he was uncertain. Days later he would ask himself if indeed he had seen the Custer Wolf. Somehow, there would have been satisfaction even in that.

By the time the white wolf had made his way, unseen and unheard, to the bottom of the hill and had slipped away toward a crack in the earth where he could hide, dusk was approaching. He had not hunted for two days because of the heat and because of an incredible instinct that told him that his pursuers were close behind.

Hunger mounted inside him, and when the first shadows were laid down across the parched earth he slipped out of his hiding place and loped toward the east and a ranch he knew well from previous raids.

After he had slipped through a barbed-wire fence, leaving yet another tuft of winter wool behind, he slowed his pace and began to take finer measurements. He knew, perhaps through instinct, perhaps through learning, that he was most vulnerable in pasture lands, for they were well watched and his own trusted nose played tricks on him in air so heavily laden with manure and urine. He kept to the inside of the fence where his outline was less discernible and began to move down toward the ranch proper. When he came to a wooden trough he slipped between it and the fence, gingerly avoiding a rattlesnake that had sought in desperation for a tolerable temperature in its shade, placed his forefeet on the rim and cautiously raised his head until he could reach the dusty surface of the water. He buried his muzzle for a moment and then began to drink, shivering as he felt the freshness of the water and flexing as the newness ran to his extremities. He sucked at the trough until he could take no more and slipped back into its shadow, his sides visibly distended. The simple addition of water had created a new wolf and he rested leisurely behind the wooden construction waiting for night to fall. From where he lay he could watch the activities of men, horses, even dogs, less than half a mile away.

When finally dark had spread itself over all and

lights had appeared in the buildings at the bottom of the pasture, the white wolf slipped free of the shadow and made his way across the pasture just below the top of the rise. Slipping through the fence on the far side, he turned his course downhill and moved through an area of brittle, dry brush. At the bottom of the hill he moved past a chicken house and heard the stirrings of the noisy ones inside, then emerged onto a broad plaza that lay open between the ranch house and a tall, parched hackberry tree. Holding back in the darkest area he watched a large dog stir from its lethargy and sniff cautiously in his direction. He sensed the rising awareness in his foe, and when he heard the first growl beginning to work its way free from the hound's throat he cut it short by the impact of his hurtling form. In three strides the white wolf was across the bare place and on top of the dog. His own involuntary fighting sounds combined with the snarling and lashing of the hound to summon a smaller dog, a terrier, hurtling into the fray from the farmhouse steps where it had been sleeping. The wolf released his hold on the hound just long enough to end the snapping terrier's life with a single bite at the base of the skull. When he turned back to the hound he was stopped by the insistence of an ancient and unexplainable ritual. The hound had slipped from his grasp, rolled over on his back and exposed his throat. The wolf, poised over the helpless animal with his anxious teeth less than an inch from the vulnerable flesh, could not bite. A wolf cannot be said to have pity, nor mercy, nor any such quality, and yet, when in combat with another of his kind (and a dog is close enough to that), he cannot sink his fangs into a throat that is offered.

The yapping terrier, in its final yelp, had summoned up activity within the house. As the front door burst open the white wolf was poised over the dog, helpless to act, held captive by an invisible force. Finally, he broke loose from his stance and streaked toward the shelter of the far side of the barn. The hound bounded after him, and from the porch the men saw it disappear behind the great building only inches behind the wolf. They heard its one long, baleful howl. Seconds later, as they cautiously approached the shadows, they heard the final pantings of the dog as it bled to death where it lay. The wolf had vanished.

Why the Custer Wolf chose, from time to time, to expose himself to the increased danger of actual barnyard raids cannot be answered. There was generally little there for him to take in the way of prey and there was no opportunity for him to eat even when he killed. It was on the high pastures—miles away from the barn, the house, and the rifle rack—that the cattle fed, the sheep grazed. There was something in the white wolf, something so perverse, that just as he would on some nights kill ten or twenty times his immediate needs, on others he was compelled to expose himself to the gravest hazards possible. It was what we would call today, in human beings, the acting out of a death-wish.

Later that night, with the death of two dogs to his

credit (but certainly not on his conscience), the Custer Wolf stopped briefly on the back pasture of another ranch ten miles distant to feed on the carcass of a colt. It was one of three horses he had killed within a space of ten minutes.

SEVENTEEN

I T was late September, 1920. In response to ancient controls and built-in clarions, each creature in the land had begun the urgent preparations for the coming change. Fall was extending its cloak of many colors over the land, offering a brief respite between the harsher seasons. The winter potential was lurking in nothing less than the movements of the planet itself. The angle at which the sun could broadcast its rays was gradually approaching the most acute, and the mornings were reflecting the difference. This rhythm's insistence pulsed to the roots and core of everything that lived. No organism could deny it and long survive.

The animals that were about to hibernate were busy

laying on their girdles of essential fat. There was little play, little left of the more frolicsome summer mood. Birds that would soon fly toward warmer places were gathering their strength, beginning to react to secret stimuli. Those animals that would stay behind and face the brutality of a southern extension of Arctic extremes were busy completing the education of the year's crop of young. Most of the young of the earth had matured to the point where their parents were about to cast them off like another season's fad, or had developed markedly reduced tolerance for their childish ways. Relatively few animals keep their young through the winter and an ageless prompting urged the final preparations. Maternal instincts were dying, fading like the summer sun.

Man, a part of the natural world despite himself, was involved in ways reminiscent of the squirrel, the bee, and the other economy-minded ones. Surplus stock was culled for market and fires burned round the clock in smoking sheds to turn flesh, which only hours before had squealed and squirmed, to sausage and loin and other gastronomic delights. Firearms crackled and slivers of metallic fire burned their way into the wildlife of the land. Bucks readying their tines and points for the tasks of battle and mate-claiming were knocked to their knees by stinging messengers of lead and the compounds of brass, steel, copper, and tin. Birds full in the sky, rich in the gift of life, were crumpled midstroke by fistfuls of hurtling pellets. Gathered up in the well-trained jaws of dogs with silken coats they were delivered pale to the feet of the gunners, there to die as time and place of pellet impact dictated. Geese were carved out of their flocks and smashed to earth by the barking guns. A bit of the sun, a bit of the wind died with each. Primitive steel tubes anchored to gunwale of punt by heavy oarlocks belched barrels of steel and debris across the otherwise quiet faces of hidden ponds. Far from the route and concern of game wardens, ducks that had answered a skillful wooden call and floated down to sit in security by the sides of judas ducks of wood were slaughtered by the truckload. A great deal of legislation was yet to be enacted and observed.

The Custer Wolf was not really a part of any of this. He could not migrate except from one ranch to another; he could not put the winter behind him in slumber beneath the ground; he had no mate to share with, no young to train, and his killing was not sanctioned. He had no smokehouse, no cannon-bored shotgun, no hunting license. He was a killer without portfolio and so was himself condemned to die.

We could search without profit in the secret byways of cause and effect and never determine if the Custer Wolf behaved as he did because of man's attitude toward him, or if man reflected in his ways only the hurt the white wolf had done. It could be argued either way with equal zeal and would always end the same: the apologist for the one would see only bad in the other. The two extremes are but mirror images of each other.

However guilt may be attributable now, the reality of that time was the fact that October was approaching and the last days of the Custer Wolf were at hand. At ten, he was prematurely tired. With perhaps no more than two thirds of a normal life lived he was beginning to show signs of slackening skill. If it was not his skill that was reduced in effectiveness, then it was his will to survive, for he was beginning to make mistakes. On one occasion a baited carcass was disturbed and the white wolf's tracks were found nearby. On another a baited lamb was nibbled at, though not eaten. He was, it appeared, becoming slower to recognize poisoned bait. The professionals squinted their eyes knowingly as they stared down at the signs written out before them and knew they were seeing the disintegration of a monumental skill. If ever during his life Lobo had one moment of human affection and regard, it was then—when the first hint of his increasing carelessness was read into the signs and marks his paws made in the matrix of dry Dakota soil. It was, however, a fleeting sympathy, for the advantage was pressed.

Toward the end, the outlaw's range began to shrink. The perimeter was reduced slowly until the smaller area enclosed made his actions slightly more predictable. The skill of the hunters who sought his pale pelt grew daily as his skill deteriorated. They sought his end before winter snows and hammering winds made the pursuit an agony of exposure and chill. All possible pressure was brought to bear and the number of traps grew with each passing day. It can truthfully be said that the Custer Wolf conquered everything he encountered in his life—except time.

His skill as a killer, his desire to kill, remained virtually unchanged to the end. But now, when the fresh news of his death was eagerly anticipated and no longer despaired of, narrowed eyes replaced flights of temper; the passion had gone out of the hunting of this wolf and he no longer made men angry. Most men, even those that hunted him professionally, never really expected to toe his carcass. There was a kind of universal feeling that one day he would just dissolve into the wilderness, victim of a poisoned fat ball, or subject of a new wanderlust. Men had so long hungered for his death that they hardly expected to witness its reality.

There now occurred a strange coincidence. H. P. Williams, it will be recalled, had succeeded earlier the same year in cutting short the career of Wyoming's fabled Split Rock Wolf. At the time, Williams had made a scent from the remains of the renegade—a scent that did not differ in kind or intensity from the scents made by scores of other hunters from as many animals in an effort to lure the white outlaw into a trap. But this had been made from the carcass of one of the worst renegade killers Wyoming had ever known, and Williams now marked a post with it—a post known to have been used by the Custer Wolf on a number of occasions. He also methodically placed yet another trap in the ground after the accepted manner, just as hundreds of other traps had been planted like so many deadly seeds along the length and breadth of the wolf's hunting range. But this one was different—and in a most important way.

People who like to make wonderful things of the permutations of chance and destiny will long continue to toy with this strange event. Perhaps any trap set that afternoon, with any scent, by any reasonably skilled hunter would have taken the Custer Wolf. Perhaps this was *the* trap, regardless of other factors. Or perhaps the Custer Wolf had simply run out of time and essential skills. Or could it have been that these two renegades, two of the last of a long line of outlaws the Western states had suffered, were meant to be joined in this strange way? They were, after all, anachronisms together—vestiges doomed by the genetics of a continent evolving into an image drawn by man.

And so this was the night, the time, the place, and the hunter. As the dark edged from the east toward the west and began pushing a day and a date into the Pacific Ocean, the night creatures of the prairies slipped from their secret places and set about the business of life. Some passed close to the yawning steel jaws that waited in the ground, but none concerned himself with them enough to relieve them of their tension. The jaws waited quietly—tensed, anointed, consecrated in the ritual of the wolf-hunter.

The Custer Wolf, too, author of a thousand useless deaths, inheritor and ignorer of an ancient and quite different animal heritage, awoke from his day's sleep and moved slowly into the stream of the night. His stomach asked for food and, perhaps, he looked forward to another night of slaughter beyond his needs. He stretched, yawned, and shook the dust from his coat.

Perhaps he laid his head back and called out that night, but there are no reports of his having done so within the range of a man's ear.

Who knows what a wolf can remember, or what he knows about himself? Perhaps, almost surely, a wolf has no awareness of self. What were the shallow dimensions of the white wolf that night when he let his left front foot bring weight to the trap's pan? How high did he jump? What kind of noises did he make and how long did he struggle?

When Williams approached the trap in the morning the white wolf lay quietly staring in his direction. His great yellow eyes responded in mute anger to the power that had instrumented his fall. Williams—involved, we may assume, in some deep and private emotion—walked toward his enemy. Perhaps he was not sure that the animal before him was even the dreaded one. Perhaps his hopes could not soar so high after so long a chase.

As Williams approached, the Custer Wolf sprang to his feet with such sudden, violent force that the trap's stake was pulled free from the ground. Despite the grinding pain that fired paralyzing spasms up into his chest and shoulder he ran—as fast, almost, as if he were unencumbered—toward a growth of stunted trees. He leaped into their midst in search of cover but was flung violently to his back and rolled over several times. The stake had caught firmly between the twin trunks of a twisted runt of a tree. At the full length of the chain he stood watching his foe approaching from the far side. The force of his weight when the stake had caught had weakened the swivel that joined the chain to the trap and, at the first tug, it parted. Free of the chain and the stake, but still encumbered by the trap, whose teeth worked deeper and more painfully into his flesh with each step he took, he turned again and ran.

It is generally conceded that the Custer Wolf ran a full three miles with the trap consuming his left front foot before Williams could get off a clear, open shot. The hunter knelt, measured his squeeze with the exquisite precision of the expert, and, as the front and rear sights of his rifle assumed the necessary relationship, a single, brittle crash parted the still morning air. At a distance of three hundred yards the white wolf took the hundred-odd grains of hurtling metal, crumpled, and lay very still. His eyes were already closed when his last, weak breath caused the slightest of disturbances in the dust at the end of his snout.

And thus, with these miniature eddies, did the life of the Custer Wolf end.

The most notable single thing about the white wolf in death, the thing that brought the most comment as his body was viewed by the dozens who came to the Richardson ranch to see for themselves, was his size. For it was an observable fact that this dread killer, this scourge of ten counties and nemesis of a hundred hunters, was a very small wolf. There was hardly a man there, and certainly no professional hunter, that had not killed bigger wolves, not once but many times.

Small, matted, white except for his crimson left front

paw, the Custer Wolf was propped up on a stake driven into the ground and photographed leaning against the leg of H. P. Williams, who in turn stood hard by the smiling rancher named Richardson. Mr. Richardson rested his right arm on Mr. Williams's left shoulder.

The photograph is old now, and a little yellow. One wonders what thoughts are behind the smiles, far behind them, and one wonders what it was in the perversity of nature that turned this small white wolf—this pale, wild canine—into the curse of a generation of ranchers and the symbol of destruction across a wide and fertile land.

ABOUT THIS BOOK

How much of what has been set down here is fact, and how much is fiction? How much, really, is known of the life of the animal known as the Custer Wolf?

In a very real sense this book is a fictionalized biography, a fact that is acknowledged without apology. The Custer Wolf did exist, he was white, and he was finally trapped and shot in October 1920, by a hunter named H. P. Williams. He was estimated to be ten years old at the time of his death and he had most definitely been one of the worst renegades this nation has ever known. The lure used by Williams is reputed to have been made from part of the notorious Split

Rock Wolf which had been killed in the same year, by the same hunter, in Wyoming. The white renegade did dig a den fifty feet deep in a draw some twenty miles beyond the Custer town limits as described in these pages. There are photographs of the site in existence. He was a mutilator as well as a wasteful killer. The recorded details of his death are substantially as reported here.

The Yearbook of the United States Department of Agriculture for 1920 carries data on the Custer Wolf, calling him by that name; writers and scientists have added bits and pieces down through the years, some of it true, some of it probably false. Stanley P. Young and Edward A. Goldman wrote a book about him, and dozens of others as well. All this material was gathered and examined before this book was written. That is one side of it: the book research.

George Wilson of St. Louis maintains a pack of full-blooded timber wolves and made his magnificent animals available to the author for study. Fortunately, I was accepted by them and was able to experience the nibbles, mouth-loving and other phenomena personally. George once slid twenty feet into a tunnel under the ground with a professional motion picture camera and a battery of lights to photograph the birth of a litter of cubs. The she-wolf trusted this remarkable man enough to allow him to return again and again to capture the first hours, days and weeks of the new wolves on film. George, with characteristic generosity, made that film available for a dozen viewings. Much of what is written

in these pages about the early life of Lobo comes from
that unique reel of film. The hours spent with Homer,
his great 135-pound pack leader, made the great tan
wolf of this story, a purely fictional "character," live
for the author. George's film, his wolves, his correspon-
dence and conversation added immeasurably to this
book.

We have been archaeologists, too, for like those pa-
tient men we have found but fragments of pottery and
have used a primitive compass to complete the perimeter of the bowl on their discernible radius. You do
not need the whole bowl, or the intact amphora, to know
the genius of Grecian potters. We have also been
paleontologists, for we have taken bits and pieces of
bone and done whole reconstructions. In that sense, our
story of the Custer Wolf is as real as the dinosaur
skeleton in the local museum.

Adolph Murie told us about the wolf, Douglas Pim-
lott did, and Lois Crisler, too. They are but a few
among dozens whose works were consulted. Some—often
all—of the things each said helped fill out the charac-
ters here constructed. I have tried to be faithful to these
observers and have attempted to present in this compos-
ite the *idealized* life story of a wolf family, specifically
in South Dakota between 1910 and 1920. The effort,
at least, has been honest when dealing with fiction as
well as with fact, and both are here admitted. To the
cardinal sin of sentimentality I confess, although I
often struggled against it.

In a way, though, when thinking and writing of the

Custer Wolf, it didn't always seem such a bad thing, this sentimentality. Perhaps I might yet be forgiven for it. And if I am not to be forgiven it, I will not care. Somehow, across the years since the blood dried and the hurt ceased to matter, I feel as if I have some slight understanding of this strange, tormented animal. One has to be sentimental about a thing like that. At least I do.

ROGER CARAS

Kew Gardens
New York

ABOUT THE AUTHOR

Roger Caras is the author of over forty books on nature, the environment, and companion animals. He is a special correspondent on those subjects for the ABC News Television Network, the only correspondent assigned full time to those topics by a network. He is also a commentator for CBS Radio on pets and wildlife and is a pet columnist for *Ladies' Home Journal*. Mr. Caras was a recent recipient of the Joseph Wood Krutch medal for "outstanding contributions to the betterment of our planet" and of the "Fido Award" as 1977's Dogdom's Man of the Year. He is an adjunct Professor of English at Southampton College; a Lecturer in Animal Biology at the School of Veterinary Medicine, University of Pennsylvania; and a Fellow of the Royal Society, London. He has been awarded a Doctor of Letters degree by Rio Grande College. Mr. Caras is married and has a son and a daughter.